Ghost Warship
of 1812

By Agnes Rodriguez Contes

Copyright 2018 by Agnes Rodriguez Contes. All rights reserved. No part of this book may be used in any form or by any means graphical, electronic, or mechanical without written permission of the copyright owner.

ISBN: 978-1-987852-16-5

First printing July 2018

Author and illustrator: Agnes Rodriguez Contes; 5 Spruce Dr., Nesconset, NY, 11767-3033; (631) 467-2180; aggiecontes@yahoo.com

Publisher: Wood Island Prints; 670 Trans-Canada Highway, RR 1; Belle River, PE C0A 1B0; (902) 962-3335; schultz@pei.sympatico.ca; www.woodislandsprints.com

Dedication

This book is dedicated to my grandchildren: Nicholas who modeled for me, Natalia, Christian, and one on the way. Also, to all future grandchildren that God may bless me with.

Facts of the War of 1812

On August 19, 1812 there were two frigates that engaged in a battle in the Atlantic Ocean somewhere between Boston-Massachusetts, and Halifax-Nova Scotia. A 'frigate' is a smaller warship that holds guns and canons. These older warships had sails like a big sail boat. The American warship, called the *Constitution*, was lead by Captain Isaac Hull, and the British warship was called the *Guerriere* lead by Captain James Richard Dacres.

When both ships began to battle, the cannon shots from the Guerriere did not penetrate the Constitution, and a soldier called the Constitution 'Iron Side'. That is how it got its nick-name, 'Old Ironsides.'

The Constitution was a much larger ship than the Guerriere with many more men. The Guerriere became badly damaged in the battle. The British had lost 21 men, with 57 wounded, including Captain Dacres who was shot in the back. He did not want any more deaths, so he raised his flag in surrender to Captain Hull. Captain Hull had lost 9 men, and 13 were wounded.

When the British crew was captured, and went on the American ship, Dacres was surprised to see British men fighting alongside the Americans. But when Dacres saw the American ship strike its colors, he dismissed the Americans in his crew from fighting against their own country, and they went to the lower deck of the ship. When the British were safe on the Constitution, Captain Hull ordered the Guerriere to be sunk because it was so badly damaged and couldn't be saved.

Both these men were brave in standing up for what they believed was right, therefore, they fought to protect their country. In their own land, many of their countrymen deemed them as heroes.

Chapter 1: Blake's Birthday

July 13, 2012 was hot and sticky; the night air was unusually stale by the beach. Blake shined a flashlight at his dusty, bronzed calves and saw them swollen from strain. He was worn out from a long hike by the seashore. Getting up early this morning had added to his fatigue. He looked up the sixty-six steep steps that led to the towering house where he lived on Five Driftwood Lane, Long Island, and decided to settle right on the beach for the night. His mother and father had already told him that when he reached twelve years old, on his birthday he could sleep by the shore. Today was that special day. Blake thought sleeping on the beach would be a rite to passage; a way to prove himself fearless and able to do just about anything, like his father.

The tall, long-haired boy glanced at his new nautical watch with built-in compass and light. "Almost midnight," he whispered. Blake dropped to his aching knees on the sand.

The beach patrolman came by, "Everything all right, son?'

Blake, in pain, rose slowly to his feet. "So far, so good. I'm out here for the first time on my own." While he talked to the patrolman, he pushed his broad chest out and his stomach in, and then stood at attention like a sailor in the Navy.

"Well then, you have yourself a good night, young man."

Blake enjoyed hearing the words echoing out of the officer's mouth 'young man'. "Thank you, and you have a good night too, officer."

The officer smiled. "Boy, you are one brave young man sleeping out here by yourself."

"Thanks," he said sheepishly, pushing back his hair. "My parents are letting me sleep here tonight. My birthday's today … I just turned twelve … and they can watch me from the house, anyhow."

"Well, that's really cool. I'll be nearby in case you need me, okay? And … Son?'

"Yeah?" said Blake.

"Happy Birthday to you, and many more."

"Thanks officer," replied Blake with a giggle and with a great big smile. He waited for the officer to move on by, so he can get comfortable.

Yawning and stretching like a cat, Blake slid his strapping, aching body along the wet ground, welcoming its coolness. The moon shone full for a while, but soon patches of dark clouds covered its light. He was too exhausted from waking up at a quarter to four in the morning to go fishing on his father's 'historical ship' purchased some weeks ago from a decrepit old sea captain, who kept a shop in the next town, east of where the deWolfes lived. He heard restless sounds of creatures lurking, but didn't give them much thought.

Blake gave a deep sigh, clasped his hands over his broad chest, and soon dozed off. Before long, Blake felt himself twist and turn like leaves blowing in an autumn wind. His legs ached; he moaned and groaned. He saw a kaleidoscope of colors dancing round and round in his head, then:

Plop! B-o-o-o-m! S-w-i-s-h! K-a-boom!

A battle! I'm in the middle of a battle! He saw sailors scurrying, and shouting, loading and firing their guns, then reloading and firing again. Blake could hear the pop of a gun and see clearly all the sailors running to

6

Chapter 1: Blake's Birthday

July 13, 2012 was hot and sticky; the night air was unusually stale by the beach. Blake shined a flashlight at his dusty, bronzed calves and saw them swollen from strain. He was worn out from a long hike by the seashore. Getting up early this morning had added to his fatigue. He looked up the sixty-six steep steps that led to the towering house where he lived on Five Driftwood Lane, Long Island, and decided to settle right on the beach for the night. His mother and father had already told him that when he reached twelve years old, on his birthday he could sleep by the shore. Today was that special day. Blake thought sleeping on the beach would be a rite to passage; a way to prove himself fearless and able to do just about anything, like his father.

The tall, long-haired boy glanced at his new nautical watch with built-in compass and light. "Almost midnight," he whispered. Blake dropped to his aching knees on the sand.

Dedication

This book is dedicated to my grandchildren: Nicholas who modeled for me, Natalia, Christian, and one on the way. Also, to all future grandchildren that God may bless me with.

Facts of the War of 1812

On August 19, 1812 there were two frigates that engaged in a battle in the Atlantic Ocean somewhere between Boston-Massachusetts, and Halifax-Nova Scotia. A 'frigate' is a smaller warship that holds guns and canons. These older warships had sails like a big sail boat. The American warship, called the *Constitution*, was lead by Captain Isaac Hull, and the British warship was called the *Guerriere* lead by Captain James Richard Dacres.

When both ships began to battle, the cannon shots from the Guerriere did not penetrate the Constitution, and a soldier called the Constitution 'Iron Side'. That is how it got its nick-name, 'Old Ironsides.'

The Constitution was a much larger ship than the Guerriere with many more men. The Guerriere became badly damaged in the battle. The British had lost 21 men, with 57 wounded, including Captain Dacres who was shot in the back. He did not want any more deaths, so he raised his flag in surrender to Captain Hull. Captain Hull had lost 9 men, and 13 were wounded.

When the British crew was captured, and went on the American ship, Dacres was surprised to see British men fighting alongside the Americans. But when Dacres saw the American ship strike its colors, he dismissed the Americans in his crew from fighting against their own country, and they went to the lower deck of the ship. When the British were safe on the Constitution, Captain Hull ordered the Guerriere to be sunk because it was so badly damaged and couldn't be saved.

Both these men were brave in standing up for what they believed was right, therefore, they fought to protect their country. In their own land, many of their countrymen deemed them as heroes.

shoot their enemy, or to hoist ropes, or to pull in canvases. Blake saw bleeding sailors with holes in their arms, legs, and stomachs. He saw lots of sailors in a state of confusion around him.

Some men wore blue woolen coats with tails and gold buttons. Their breeches were tan and tied right below their knees. They wore black leather boots, high enough to reach the edge of their breeches. These men are dressed in British uniform. *I'm on a British ship!* Blake interrupted a sailor wearing a white cotton shirt and gray trousers on the deck, "Hey, soldier. Where am I?"

"Have Ye been hit? Where are ye bleeding, boy?"

"No, I don't know where I am. Can you please tell me?"

"Laddie, ye've lost yer mind. Ye've must've bumped yer head or something must have dropped on ye. Ye're here on the Royal Navy Ship!"

Blake repeated, "The Royal Navy Ship?"

"Yes, lad. The HMS Guerriere. It is one of our finest Royal Navy Ships. Now grab a weapon!"

Blake looked around wildly. "Hey Mister, that ship?" he asked another sailor. "Whom are you fighting?"

The sailor spit through the space between his rotten teeth. "Lad ye better pick up yer musket. Just be sure it has been popped or it'll blow up in yer face. They are the Americans. The famous American Frigate Constitution we are fighting! That ship's a monster!"

Ka-boom! Boom! Rat-a-tat-tat. Boom!

"We pelt the hull from our broadside and those pelts bounce right off. That ship ain't no ship lad, she has the sides of iron. For the life of me, I've never seen such a thing! It is a monster, I tell ye! Now pick up yer musket and shoot!" one sailor rattled on.

"Get that man over there!" a sailor shouted, pointing at an American standing on the deck of his own ship.

Another cried, "Take in the topsails and jib!"

Yet another shouted, "Pull in the Fore-topmast staysail too!" But when a sailor pulled one of the ropes, the man shouted to the sailors below. "Watch for the canvas falling!"

Blake, looking up, watched in horror as the canvas fell right on top of a sailor, snapping his neck.

B-o-o-o-m! "A cannonball just hit our mizzenmast!" shouted a British sailor.

Splash went another cannonball into the sea. *Rat-a-tat-Boom! Splash!* Men scurried about on the deck. One looked at Blake fiercely, "Our main yard just has been shot away! Boy, pick up a gun and start shootin'!"

"A gun! But I've never shot a gun before," replied Blake.

"Boy, do ye want to live? Well then, by shootin' is how ye live! Now shoot, boy!"

The sailor wore a black patch over an eye, which Blake thought made him appear evil. Whether or not he was really evil, Blake did not know. On the same sailor's blue coat, a gold button dangled and shimmered with a glint of sunlight, which caught Blake's eye. Confused, Blake cocked the trigger and shot in the direction of where the cannon ball had destroyed the mizzenmast. *B-a-n-g!*

Blake fell back. "My arm!"

"Are ye shot up, boy?"

"No, I think I hurt my arm while trying to shoot this stupid thing. But, I don't feel it." Blake was puzzled.

The soldier with the patch grabbed Blake's arm, and shoved him to the side of the ship. "Boy this is war, get up and fight like a man!"

But my Dad doesn't shoot a gun, Blake thought. *And my Dad is a man. I want to be like him, not what you think I should do or who I should be.*

Blake snapped back in time to see the ship crumble right before his eyes. The rest of the mizzenmast crashed into the sea, and other parts onto the deck leaving nothing but a stump. Blake dodged from harm's way. *But I'm twelve and never shot a gun before.*

Blake smelled the stale air. What's that awful stench? It smells of rotting flesh. Blake looked all around him. *Why is part of this ship on fire?* "*FIRE!!!*" he yelled, but no one seemed to hear him anymore. The stench grew worse. A mist began to hover over them, over the ship, over the sea.

Blake knew that the captain of the other ship ordered thunderous shots of musketry and broadside continuously in the misty weather. The sound was as if packs of firecrackers were lit all at the same time. The British ship suffered much damage.

Wherever Blake went on deck, the old and weathered planks cracked and creaked under his feet. He went through one. "My foot is caught!" he shouted. "This ship is sinking, on fire, and it's rotting!" Blake looked around for help. All he saw were the tattered sails, the holes on deck, what was left of the masts smoldering with fire, and not one soul. The ship tilted to one side and began to sink. Just then, he felt himself lift off the ground, twisting and twirling in an array of kaleidoscopic colors and fell into an uncertain place.

Blake was abruptly awakened by a strong sound of flapping wings. "What was that?!" he exclaimed, broadening his eyes to see the dull light of the misty dawn. He was back on the beach. He felt the harsh north wind across his face, pushing back the strands of dampened hair.

"*B-l-a-k-e. B-l-a-k-e,*" called a trembling voice.

"Who's calling me?" he asked, jerking his strong neck to look behind him. He scanned the sandy area with half-sleepy eyes, not seeing anyone. Blake could hear and feel the hard thump in his bare chest. "I must not be awake yet," he mumbled, stumbling to his feet. "I must still be dreaming. But the voice sounded so real."

Suddenly, stronger gusts of wind blew off the sea. "*B-l-a-k-e! B-l-a-k-e!*" he heard several voices this time. Frightened, Blake staggered toward the thicket. The thorns of a wild rose bush sliced open his muscular calf.

Maybe it's Mom calling me, he tried to reason. Blake, his leg bloodied, started up the sixty-six, sun bleached, splintered wooden steps, up the bluffs toward home. At the top, a tall shadowy figure stepped from behind the towering blue spruce into Blake's path. "Aaaahhhh!!!"

"Are you all right?" spoke the silhouette of a man Blake recognized. "Dad. It's only you," he said in relief. "Dad. I had a weird dream. Then I heard the winds call my name."

Just then the beach patrolman came around from the lower cliff shouting up to Captain deWolfe and Blake, "Is everything all right?"

"Yes officer, everything is fine. He has the jitters, that's all."

"All right, then I'll leave you folks and head over to the base. Have a good day." The officer tipped his hat and disappeared.

Captain deWolfe turned to Blake. "Look. It's just your imagination. You've always been a young man of adventure. That's why your mother and I decided to let you sleep by the shore."

"Really, Dad," Blake said in his raspy, sure voice. "The wind actually called my name. I'm as sure of it as I am sure you're standing in front of me."

Captain deWolfe peered closely at Blake. "Son, we'll talk more … and what happened to your leg? The blood is running into your water shoes. Better take care of that when you get inside the house."

Entering the hollow corridor of the deWolfe mansion, they were met by yet another disheveled figure dragging something behind, making hideous echoing sounds.

Blake still jittery from his nightmare, panicked. He tugged on the Captain's blue denim shirt. "Dad! Turn on the light, hurry—Mom!" Blake cried out.

Blake's mother, half-asleep in her robe, walked toward them, her slippers scuffing the floor. "What's going on? Are you all right? I heard someone screaming, so I jumped out of bed." Mother noticed Blake's leg. "Blake you're bleeding!"

The captain answered in a deep tone, "We're fine I think, Elizabeth." Then he turned to her, and Blake heard the captain whisper, "Blake might be a bit spooked though. He claims to have heard his name being called by the wind."

Blake felt his face flush. "Dad, I'm not joking! I really heard it."

Captain motioned with his hands, "Blake, calm down. I'm only explaining to your mother what you told me. I believe you."

Elizabeth's dark eyebrows jumped, exposing a look of disbelief. "I think you boys need some hot chocolate. Hot cocoa is good for your soul all year round. And Blake, go get cleaned up and bandage your leg tightly to stop the bleeding. Then go talk in the library. I lit a fire in the fireplace, when I heard some noises thinking that you two might end up in there."

His mother gave a big yawn, then said, "Strange how, on this summer day, it turned chilly when the wind began to blow. Hmm, I don't get it. Well, I'll bring the cocoa in there too." She headed for the kitchen, tying the strings of her robe and shaking her head.

Chapter 2: Nightmare

Walking toward the mahogany double doors of the library, Blake turned to his father. "What do you know about the warship you bought from that sleazy Mr. DeMarcus a few weeks ago?"

"Don't talk that way. How do you know he's sleazy?" Blake apologetically said, "Sorry, Dad."

"I'm not quite sure I know everything about the ship. One thing I do know is that it was in a battle. It fought with the USS Constitution in the Atlantic Ocean, east of Boston in the war of 1812," captain deWolfe paused. "But, there seems to be something fishy going on. For some reason, whenever I repair a plank, it seems that the new plank might be water damaged already, or it decays quickly. I can't figure out why it's happening."

"Dad. You just said our ship was in battle with a ship called the USS Constitution?" Blake's eyes were glued on his father while he paced the floor. He had some doubt that his father's ship might have been the very ship to be in battle with American ship, but anything was possible.

The captain paused to pull a mahogany pipe with a carving of a ship at sea round its bowl from the fireplace mantel. It was given to him as a gift from his father a few years back before he died. The captain was a man who loved the sea and all sorts of things connected to it, and this one pipe he did cherish.

"Yes, why do you ask?" He lit his pipe and took several puffs to get it going.

"You're not going to believe this, but I think the dream I had was about the ship you bought and the American Constitution. It must be the same ship you're talking about. One of the sailors in my dream called it the American Frigate Constitution. I also asked another sailor where I was, and he said, 'The Royal Navy Ship, The HMS Guerriere.'"

Captain deWolfe threw the match into the fireplace. The blue smoke from his pipe began to climb, filling the room with a cherry tobacco scent. The captain turned and gazed deeply into Blake's eyes. Hesitantly he said, "Supposedly, that ship sank. The Constitution tore it to pieces. But I don't know for sure."

"Dad, in my dream it did sink," Blake sighed. "How can it sail now?" Blake puckered his lips as he usually did when trying to figure something out, pacing the polished, wooden floor, just like his father did a moment ago.

Captain deWolfe, now in front of a wall of books, sitting in a chair that resembled a captain's chair on a yacht, turned to Blake and said, "The ship is said to have belonged to the French. Then in one of the battles, the British took it from the French, and it was British property ever since—until now that is. It fought in the Atlantic Ocean, east of Boston on the 19th of August 1812. It is said that on every August 19th since then, a white mist has been spotted in the very place of the battle. I believe it is just a legend." The captain stood up from his chair and turned toward the fireplace of burning birch, throwing another log into it.

Blake asked again, "But how is it now running if it was broken into pieces, on fire, and sunk into the Atlantic Ocean?"

"How do you know it was on fire?" asked the captain.

"I saw it all in my dream."

"Well, legend has it that somehow in the mist, the ship was rebuilt." He turned and walked toward the huge wall of windows overlooking the sea where Blake stood.

Blake's eyes were fixed out of the opened window. He saw the black sea pounce on the huge boulders and heard the waves clap and roar against the rocks. "Dad. That's impossible. Aren't you scared?"

"No, not really." Puffing away, he glanced toward Blake, and looked out the window again. "I'm a ship mechanic and the best in my field. People send for me from across Long Island Sound and pay me top dollar to do work on their sea-crafts. I know I can rebuild the ship strongly. I liked the way it looked, and I'm intrigued by history—as you already know—therefore, I purchased the ship."

Just then, "Hot chocolate?" interrupted Elizabeth, entering the library.

"Thanks, Mom," Blake said, then changed the subject a bit. "Oh, by the way, thank you both for throwing that party for me yesterday. And Dad, the fishing trip was fun on that big old ship, even if it needs to be repaired."

"You're welcome, son," said his mother and father at the same time, smiling at Blake.

"And thanks for trusting me to sleep on the beach. Even though strange things happened." Blake cringed all over again at the thought of the night's event. He stared into his cup that swirled a mist off the brown, hot liquid and took a sip, not feeling any better. Blake thought by acting more like his father, he would feel good inside. "Dad, what are you thinking? I know there are other things on your mind. Want to share them?"

"As a matter of fact, I do. Blake, you are adventurous. I want you to do something for me—investigate the history of the ship and see what you can come up with. The name of the ship you dreamt of was called the Guerriere, right?"

"Yeah," said Blake.

"Okay, since I'm booked with appointments for a month, I don't have much time right now to research the ship. I want you to do it for me. Is that all right with you?"

Blake lifting his eyebrow, creasing his forehead slightly, "All right, Dad. But, what if I can't find information on the ship other than what we already know?"

The captain put his strong hand on Blake's shoulder and stared into his eyes. "Son, I have great confidence that you will." He turned and walked out the door.

This was Blake's first direct mission from the captain. Blake felt like a true sailor and said, "Aye-aye Captain," while respectfully saluting his father, already going down the hallway.

All day Blake thought about the dream he'd had and the voices he'd heard early that morning by the seashore. Not knowing where the voices came from, he began to think that maybe someone was playing some dirty tricks on him. Then he spoke his thought aloud, "Perhaps those voices were all in my mind after all?" Blake had a mind for adventure that wandered in every direction except straight.

Although he was usually not afraid of much, it was almost embarrassing how frightening this experience was for Blake. Blake was tall and brawny like his father, his forearms well built from helping the captain set sails since he was five. He was determined to follow in his father's footsteps and that included bravery. For Blake, his dad was his hero. Whatever his dad asked of him, he would do it to his fullest until the job was done. Blake knew that the captain was to take him to begin his investigation on the old ship early the next morning. But, for right now, he decided to rest and not think anymore. Blake ate dinner, washed up, and set his alarm clock for 5:30 A.M. to beat the fisherman's rush on the docks. His father had to be across the sound by 7:30 that morning for work. He went to bed early that night to have enough rest for the next day's events.

Chapter 3: First Visit to DeMarcus

"Gooood-Morrrr-ning to everyone out there who is just waking up with us this fine morning," blared his radio. "Iiit'sss-going to be-another lovely, warm day. Great for fishing for all you folks who get up this early...."

Blake's eyes opened and saw that it was 5:30. I can't believe it's morning already, he thought while pushing his lose hair off his face. He quickly hit the huge off button on his bright white clock radio and threw aside his sheet. He swung both legs off one side of his bed and pushed himself up. Making his way toward the window, he grabbed his navy blue and yellow striped pants and blue tee shirt that read, 'Do Not Fear' that the church youth sold as a fund-raiser.

Blake looked out into the ocean. Something was in the distance. Playfully, he thought maybe there is such a thing as enormous sea creatures after all. Taking a harder look, he questioned that thought. There was a strange light in the middle of the ocean. What was it? He didn't have much time to fall into a deep speculation. Today he was to investigate the historical ship his father had bought from an old sea captain, not far from where they lived on eastern Long Island.

Blake tiptoed into his parent's room, careful not to wake his mother and shook Captain deWolfe while whispering in his ear, "Dad, get up. You said you were going to drive me. It's nearly six o'clock in the morning, and if we don't hurry it up, the docks will be filled with fishermen. I can't investigate peacefully once it gets crowded."

Working so closely with his dad, he knew more about sailing, fishing, and about the sea in general than some of the fishermen. Blake tiptoed back into his bedroom. While waiting for the captain, he lay back down on his bed. He crossed his arms behind his head, crossed his feet with his sneakers that were partly hanging off the side of the bed, and his mind began to drift. He deeply eyed the ceiling, and right when he was thinking of the beach, his father interrupted his thoughts.

"Blake, are you ready?" his father called out from the kitchen to the adjacent room, snapping Blake back into reality. "We've got to go."

Blake jumped right up. "I'm coming."

The captain finished his coffee, grabbed his sandy beige windbreaker and met Blake in the corridor. "Today is a big day. Are you excited?"

"Oh, I sure am. What do you suppose I'll find?"

"I hope you can find something that we don't already know. Somehow, I feel that there is a mystery attached to this ship and I can't put my finger on it. In searching, maybe you can find what it is. Do you understand?"

"I think so. I'll try my best, Dad."

"I know you will. Lock the door before closing it, and don't slam it." Beginning their short journey a few miles east of where they lived, they both got into the vehicle, and the black Hummer pulled away from their driveway bordered with a hedge of red and white azaleas. They pulled up a long dirt pathway with huge old maple, oak, and pine trees that towered over its path, kicking up a brown cloud behind them. At the end of the very long driveway it was suddenly becoming foggy. "Okay, son. I'll drop you off, but you'll have to walk home. I've got to be in Connecticut in an hour and a half to fix some guy's tug. It will take me a little over an hour to sail across the Sound, then to work on that man's vessel. I'll be gone for hours today."

"Thanks for driving me here."

"Blake." The captain paused and stared into Blake's eyes. "Be careful, and I love you."

Blake was a thoughtful young man. Smiling, Blake hugged his dad and said, "I love you too, Dad. Now go before you make yourself late. I'll be just fine ... I promise." Blake walked the rest of the way toward the creepy cabin of Mr. DeMarcus, also known as, 'The Coast Guard Station at Greenville Seaport of Long Island'. It was a little wooden shack with planks half falling off its sides. A rusty nail on either side of the wooden planks held each one up, and some loose ones danced every time a gust of wind went by. It needed an extensive renovation job just like the Guerriere.

When Blake entered the dilapidated shack, he was met by a foul stench all too familiar to him. The face of the old sea captain who stared down at Blake, was also vaguely familiar. He was strangely dressed in a dusty, woolen, high-collar, navy blue coat with tails. The second of its round tarnished metal buttons was missing. He resembled the man with the eye patch in Blake's nightmare only this man didn't have a patch. DeMarcus' filthy breeches were frayed. He wore worn-out-black leather boots up to his knees. He was hunched over a bit, and Blake thought, maybe the old man had been shot like the sailor in his dream.

His hair was dirty, gnarled, and matted like a long-haired dog that never got brushed. Blake walked cautiously toward the counter and saw that the man was a foot shorter than he. "Mr. DeMarcus. Um, I need to know about the ship you sold to my dad a few weeks ago." Blake felt uneasy, unsure of what to tell the pitiful looking man, so pale and thin, who stood in front of him. Blake could feel his hands sweat.

Mr. DeMarcus faced Blake. "What about the frigate?" He spoke in a croaky voice.

Blake began to wonder if he should be there without his father. "Well, I've experienced strange things since my dad bought the ship a few weeks ago."

"What sort of strange things?"

The smell of rot was so intense in the cabin that Blake felt faint and nauseous. He began to tremble, trying to figure out this prune-faced man with one green glass eye at half-mast. Blake hugged himself for comfort. "I keep hearing someone call my name, but no one's around."

The man began to laugh like a lunatic. He danced around crazily, singing, "They're coming! They'll be free! They've found ye!"

Mr. DeMarcus lunged toward Blake while pointing his filthy, bony finger an inch from Blake's eyes. It reminded him of a girl from school named Melissa who once pointed her accusing finger at him in the schoolyard, only this was much more uncomfortable, strange, and frightening.

Blake could not speak. The dreariness, the stench, the insanity on DeMarcus' face all made his blood run cold. He ran out of the damp, clammy coast guard's cabin, not wanting to look back.

He entered the neighborhood candle shop called "Sweet Scent." Sara, who ran the shop, had a welcoming smile. She had taken a liking to Blake some months ago when she first moved into the neighborhood from Ennis, County Clare, Ireland. Blake would talk to her about historical places, including her hometown. Her skin was pale with freckles. Her eyes danced every time she spoke. Her hair was long, silky brown with some red highlights in it. The beautiful creature asked, "Are you all right, Blake?" in her Irish accent, pulling her shawl over her shoulders. "Who are you runnin' from?" She softly, placed one hand on his shoulder to settle him.

When Sara touched him, he gained strength to speak. "No one. Really. I just need to catch my breath, that's all."

With her warm smile, she said, "Okay then, you may stay as long as you like."

As she turned away, Blake could smell the sweet scent of floral perfume, which made him think of a funeral. Suddenly, it all came back to him like a recurring nightmare in his mind. He felt the pain in his gut. DeMarcus' green glass eye at half-mast; his decaying, discolored teeth; the horrifying stench of rotting flesh; the dampness and clamminess of the cabin, all the weirdness. It all began to sink deep into Blake's head like a horrible nightmare that had come true; then again, he began to tremble with fear. Soon, Blake composed himself and continued toward home.

The hour-long walk seemed to take forever. When Blake entered through the massive doors, he noticed the mansion was empty and quiet. The only noise was the slamming of the door behind him that echoed in the corridor. He entered the kitchen to get some iced-tea. There on the message-board was, *Went shopping. See you later, Mom.* Blake wanted someone to talk to—someone who would hear his rambles about all that had happened. This time, he did not welcome the empty, quiet place. His mind continued to rewind and replay the scenes from the coast guard's station.

That evening after dinner, Blake went down to the shore where he heard the whispers of his name. He thought about last year's episode with a girl in his class that he'd teased so badly by putting worms in her new water bottle and wondered, *Perhaps God is punishing me for what I've done to Melissa. Or maybe Melissa is the one who is playing this dirty trick on me to get me back?* Was it Melissa, his imagination, or something else? He glanced at the tee shirt he put on that morning: *Do Not Fear.* Those words somehow brought strength to Blake, maybe because he'd bought the shirt at church, or maybe it reminded him of scripture he had to memorize when going to Sunday school. In any case, he bravely sat on the beach, dipping his feet into the water and waited to hear the voice or voices again.

Chapter 4: The Voices

An hour passed, and Blake's eyes grew heavy. Feeling sleepy, he lay on the cool, wet sand. From his canvas satchel he pulled out the brand-new pair of binoculars his grandmother had given him for his birthday and an oil lamp. In the satchel's side pocket was a book of damp matches. After striking almost all of them, he finally lit the lantern and placed his things a yard away. He had almost dozed off when, from the northeast, a strange breeze began to blow a haze his way. "*B-l-a-k-e. B-l-a-k-e! We need you,*" a voice cried out in the misty wind. Blake sat up, shook his head, and cleared the sand from his eyes.

This time, he answered the voice, "What do you want from me?"

"*You have to set us free.*".

"Free from what?"

"*We need rest.*"

"Rest. Rest from what? How?"

There was no answer. He threw up his arms and shrugged his shoulders. "Rest from what? Free from what? I don't get it!" The voice had vanished. "Oh-come-on!" Blake picked up a rock and threw it into the ocean. "Answer me!" Blake shouted hopelessly.

In a strange way, Blake felt discouraged that the unexplained voice in the wind didn't answer him back. Blake stood staring into the blackness of the sea. Before long, his eyes widened in distress. In the midst of the dark waters appeared a white shadow that continued to grow. With his binoculars he saw a huge ship with tattered sails. He couldn't believe his eyes. *I know that can't be dad, because he's already had come back from Connecticut and he's in the house.*

Blake gathered his things quickly and ran home, being careful not to turn off the oil lantern, yet tripping over his own feet. Busting through the huge front double doors and slamming them behind him, out of breath he cried out, "Dad! Dad! Come quickly. There is a ship out there you need to see."

Elizabeth came running toward the corridor. "Blake, you almost broke the door." She broke off when she saw the horrified look on his face. Grasped by fear for him, she quickly stopped, put her hand to her chest, and gasped for air.

Blake's father came out of his study. "What is it, son? You're as white as a ghost." Then the captain's eyes examined Blake up and down. Reaching toward him, Captain deWolfe said, "Slow down and tell me what frightened you?"

Still gasping for air, Blake finally began to speak, "In the water—a big ship—come see!" That was all he could say, The captain and Blake grabbed their binoculars and the still-lit lantern and, in their bare feet, ran down the long wooden steps through the thicket to spy on the ship, with Elizabeth running right behind. A warm, summer, salty breeze blew

Blake's hair, pushing the limp strands of out of his face.

"Oh, my goodness—look at that white cloud in the ocean—umm, but that's all I see Blake," said captain deWolfe.

"I told you Dad! Didn't I tell you there is something out there?" All fidgety, Blake was bouncing up and down. They both looked through their own binoculars toward the mist. In his squeaky, raspy voice, he said, "Dad, it's right there. Don't you see it?"

"No, I don't." Captain deWolfe examined his binoculars, and then said, "Perhaps mine are broken. Let me look through yours." The captain took Blake's big, black, bulky binoculars and examined it too.

For a split second, Blake thought that his father looked spooky when he quickly disguised himself by putting the black rims to his eyes.

"No. I still can't see it. Blake, are you sure you see something that resembles a ship?"

Blake's mind snapped back to the beach. "Let me look again." Blake excitedly snatched the binoculars from his father's hands and focused on the mist. "I can see the tall ship with tattered sails!"

The captain turned to Blake and grabbed his shoulders. "Son, tell me everything that happened to you, but first, I want you to slow down. Do you hear me? Catch your breath, speak slowly. Now again, tell me what happened."

Blake glanced at his Mom and saw her fear. Then he saw her look up and heard her say, "Dear God. You've created all things. You know what's troubling Blake. Please Lord, help him."

Blake took a deep, steady breath through his nose, and exhaled slowly through his mouth several times to purge his anxiety. "Okay, okay. I told you. The winds called me. You already know that part. They say I need to set them free. But they didn't say from what. I also spoke to Mr. DeMarcus. He scared me."

"Did he say anything significant?"

"As a matter of fact, he did. First, he said, 'They're coming. They'll be free', and that they have found me. But who's they? What does it mean?" Blake paused a moment, then continued. "Then Mr. DeMarcus began laughing at me like a demon, and the place smelled of rotting flesh. It was awful. I was so scared, I ran out the door." Blake felt helpless, ashamed. His eyes filled with water.

"Did you learn anything about the ship?"

"No," whispered Blake, feeling upset, worthless that he didn't learn any additional information about the historical ship—'the frigate' as DeMarcus called it—the Guerriere.

"Blake, don't let one incident get you down. Tomorrow you and I will together pay Mr. DeMarcus a visit. I'm canceling all my appointments. Let's go home." The captain blanketed Blake and Elizabeth's shoulders with his arms.

They entered the house, right toward the kitchen. Elizabeth spoke in a soft tone to break the spooky feeling that had come over them all.

"Hey. I'll go make us some snacks and we'll go sit in the dining room and talk about some good ol' times. Does that sound good to you?" Elizabeth always tried to remedy a negative situation with a positive one.

"Honey, that sounds really good to me. How about you, Blake? Are you up to that?"

Blake wasn't sure. He had mixed feelings about everything. He thought about it for a minute then, "What the heck, I'm in." He agreed, but not really wanting to do it.

"Well then, you boys move yourselves into the feasting area, and I'll be out shortly with the goodies." Motioning with her hands, Elizabeth swept the Captain and Blake out of the kitchen.

The dining area was a huge room with few furnishings in it. It had a high ceiling, polished oak-wood floors, and a large picture window on one full wall, with two oil paintings on opposite sides of the walls. One painting had brilliant colors of the ocean at sunset, and the other of the nearby lighthouse with its marvelous beacon lights at dusk. The windows were opened and screened. The view of the sea was breathtaking. In the sea's darkness you could see the dim lights of sailing ships, yachts, small boats as well as brighter lights from larger ones. The lighthouses flashed their bright lights every seven seconds. From inside the mansion you could smell the salt water. The waves were slapping madly against the black, stone jetty, and the roar was hypnotizing. The cranberry-red walls in this grand room echoed when one spoke, and so did the sound of the roaring sea.

"Dad, the sea sounds so peaceful. In a way, I feel as if the waves and the sea are calling me. But I don't actually hear voices right now other than real people speaking to me." Blake chuckled at all the weirdness, and then got serious again. "Dad, tell me the truth. Do you think I'm going crazy? What's happening to me? I just don't get it."

The captain gave his son a deep stare. "No. But honestly, I think you have a vivid imagination. And you are a very bright young man. You are a hard worker and dare to do the impossible. And usually, you're not one to be afraid of things."

Elizabeth at that moment entered the room. She walked in with a tray of tea sandwiches, cookies, coffee for the captain and herself, and iced-tea for Blake. She set it in the middle of a huge cherry wood table. Around the table sat high-back padded chairs. Blake and his father sat in two, leaving the middle chair empty for Elizabeth.

"Well, are you guys ready for some good, comforting stories?" She plopped herself between them while speaking. Blake knew Mother would want to sit herself between them where she could grab either of their arms if she had to. That was always Mom's way. Looking to comfort someone who needed it, more than to receive it. All three had a lovely view of the sea in front of them.

"Well, Blake. Did you enjoy your party the other day?"

"Yes, Mom. I really did."

For a moment, no one spoke. "Blake," said Mother. "I remember watching you and your father walk down the docks. You must have been about five years old, with the cutest golden curls I've ever seen on a little boy. You would dress like him too," she pointed toward the captain. "You wore jeans, brown dock shoes, and a white tee shirt. When the sun got too hot, you were ready with your white shorts, just like your dad. You would take off your socks and wear your shoes without them. You even changed your tee shirt into a tank top. You never had left his side, not even for a moment. You always tried to prove that you could do the things he did. One day you were given the job to pull in long heavy ropes from the sails and put them in a pile, and you struggled, but the job was done correctly. I also remember, the moment you came home, you had to get your basketball and start shooting, tired as you were."

Mom paused, took a sip of her coffee and smiled. "You loved playing basketball with your father, too. As you got older, you played very well in the little leagues. I thought you would grow out of the game after a while, but you never did. Now I see you are growing up. You've maintained good grades in school, still love basketball, and you still work well with your dad. How many boys your age can show that?"

Blake, giving his parents a wonderful complement in the midst of craziness said, "I had great teachers. You and Dad are the best teachers I know."

Blake was surprised that his mother did most of the talking that night. She was one who usually kept opinions to herself. He also knew what his mother was saying was true. For a moment, Blake felt his heart swell with delight, with joy, with courage.

After a long pause, the captain slapped his knee and said, "Well, what do you say we turn in, so we can get an early start in the morning?"

Blake felt his heart flutter like a raven's wing fighting to catch its prey. He heaved a deep sigh. "What time are we getting up?"

"If we get up at six o'clock, that would give us plenty of time. Remember, I'm not going to work tomorrow."

"Okay, Dad. I'll wash up and hit the sack now so that in the morning I can think a little more clearly. Love ya, Dad."

Blake turned to his mother, "Mom, thanks. I think I'm going to need lots of good memories, so I don't become so rattled. Maybe I can sleep better tonight too."

Blake felt the compassion coming from Elizabeth's eyes. "Good night. I'll see you in the morning. Blake '"

"Yeah."

"I love you."

"Love you too, Mom, and thanks for having faith in me. Good night."

Blake turned into his room, pulled his black leather chair in front of the huge window and looked intently toward the sea. He sat for hours thinking of all that had happened. Why didn't the wind answer me back? *I can't believe it; Dad could not see what I saw, just the mist. How can that be, that Dad could not see the ship? Maybe I am going mad after all.* Blake wondered how tomorrow would be. His imagination ran wild, and the words *Rest* and *Free* kept playing in his mind like a catchy jingle that wouldn't go away.

Blake looked at his watch. Wow. It's already one o'clock. *How in the world am I going to get up at six? I better try to sleep.* Blake abruptly got up off his chair and threw open a window wider. *Man, I feel like I'm in a wind tunnel ready to get sucked out.* He walked over to his bed, ran his fingers through his hair, then plopped right in it, still dressed, moaning and groaning. He stared at the high ceiling, hoping to doze off quickly. The smell of the salty water, and the sound of the waves began to drift through the open window. Like a lullaby, it began to lull him to sleep, then into the state of unconsciousness, into a dream world.

Blake twisted and turned, moaned and groaned. Every muscle in his body wanted to relax, but his mind was going full speed ahead.

Half asleep, he felt as if he was in a vacuum, seeing an array of colors, twisting and twirling, falling into nothingness. He was dropped in utter blackness. Then he heard, *thump-thump, thump-thump*. The sounds were getting closer and faster *thump-thump-thump-thump*. Blake was running, but running from what? He saw a fog and dim lighting afar off. Good, there is someone that can help me. As Blake ran deeper into the fog toward the shadowy person, it looked hunched over, with wild hair, then, "Aaaahhhh!!!" He woke up in the middle of it right before the semi-human face was revealed.

He woke up in a sweat—his heart ticking fast like the second hand on a clock.*What is happening to me?* Blake got himself out of bed, *I had another nightmare. When is it all going to end?*

At the other end of the long hallway, there was a sunken room where the sports channel always played on their huge TV screen. Blake had been allowed to pick out the decor of that room. Anyone could tell that blue was his favorite color, and that basketball was his favorite sport. Blake happened to be one of the top five players in his school too. The den had curtains with basketball patterns on them, and a basketball wall clock that hung on a dark blue wall. Halfway up the wall, it was decorated with basketball wallpaper, with a thick white wooden trim where the paper met the painted wall.

Blake went into the den, hoping that reading the sports section in the newspaper would settle him a bit. After a while, he looked at the basketball den's wall clock to see it a little past three in the morning. *I've got to try to get some rest. I thought I would be able to sleep tonight, but I guess the fun memories didn't work all that well.* Blake closed the paper, got up from the plush orange couch, and stood at the entrance looking in with his hand on the switch. *Good night den, maybe I'll see you in a little while, or maybe I'll fall asleep for three hours. Who knows? And why do I keep talking to myself?* Blake shrugged his shoulders, turned off the light, returned to his room, and plopped himself back on his bed staring at his ceiling once again. Before long, he fell into a deep, deep sleep.

Chapter 5: Captain Meets DeMarcus

Early the next morning, Blake said to his dad, "I really feel like I'm losing it. It's just that I've never thought such crazy stuff before. Is this what it means—growing up? If so, it really stinks!"

"Blake, we will investigate and find out why all of this is happening. There must be a logical explanation. If we knew the history of the ship, it would help solve this mystery. You're not losing it, Blake. Just hang in there. You've got to trust me."

Blake talked in a frustrated tone," I do, D-a-d. Are we set to go?" "If you're ready, I'm ready. Let's go."

They quietly left the house, got into the vehicle, and drove away. Before long, the captain drove up the dirt path that led to the graveled parking lot of the Greenville Seaport. He drove slowly, looking around strangely, and said, "Blake, do you see a heavy fog around the coast guard station or is it dust in my eyes?"

"This is strange. It doesn't seem to be anywhere else but by the station."

After Captain deWolfe parked his black Hummer, they got out of the vehicle, walked in haste toward the building, and went through the old plank door that creaked on its rusty hinges. There were pulleys, ropes of all sizes, nuts and bolts and canvases for the sailing ships. Approaching the unpolished wooden counter, the captain said, "Mr. DeMarcus, what can you tell me about the ship I bought from you?"

Grinning wide, exposing his greenish-brown decaying teeth, Mr. DeMarcus said, "Why?"

"Strange things have been happening, and I want to get to the bottom of it, that's why."

"Has it happened to you?" Mr. DeMarcus asked, pointing his crooked thin finger with a dirt-filled fingernail in the captain's face.

"No. But to my son," replied the captain through his teeth.

"Then your son has to set them free," replied the decrepit sea captain, swinging his head to look at Blake with his glass eye half-shut.

Blake felt his gut twist. "What do you mean? How do I do that? What do you want me to do?" he questioned the old man scared half to death.

"You need to go to the Ghost Ship and locate the bones of the thirteen men. Then you need to take their remains to British territory and lay them to rest there."

"Who are these men? Do you know their names?"

The shriveled old man let out a shrieking laugh that sent chills up Blake's back, and at that moment, he realized the mission was going to be much harder than he expected.

"One is called Blake deWolfe." He laughed again, an evil sound. "That's all I know, that's all I can tell ye for now." Still laughing, he slithered out the door and disappeared into the dense fog.

Those words sent an ice-cold chill through Blake's blood that he held his stomach tightly. "Dad! One sailor has my name! How could that be possible?" cried Blake. "And that word he used, 'Ye.' I've heard that before. He reminds me of the first dream I had." Every part of Blake pulsated. He could feel his heart beating in his chest, as if a drum was being played inside of him. Blake's eyes drifted toward the ceiling. Ready to faint, he felt his father's powerful hands clutch his arms to keep him from hitting the floor. Blake took a few seconds then shook his head. "I'm all right Dad, really. I'm okay now."

"Blake, I don't know how a sailor has your name, but we'll find out. I promise." Captain deWolfe helped Blake out of the horrifying cabin, and into the vehicle, then started the engine, and off they drove toward home.

When they reached home, the captain made Blake go into his bedroom to take it easy for a while. To his surprise, Blake slept for almost five hours. After Blake awoke in the afternoon, still feeling heavily burdened, he dragged his feet toward the captain's study. The captain was ready to discuss the next step to solving the mystery.

"Blake, I think we need to do some research at the Maritime Library in Utter Ville. Hopefully that will reveal some clues."

Blake felt his eyes hot and heavy from worry. He gave his father a blank stare, and then turned away, not saying a word. The evils of that day twisted in his mind.

He slid his shaking hands over his face and said to himself, *Why was I chosen to do this? Why do the voices call me? Why does one have my name? Why is such a curse on me? I don't get the whole thing, but I know I'll find out soon, real soon.*

Chapter 6: Library Research

A week went by, and Blake did not hear the voices. As he lay in bed one morning, his mind was a bit more at ease. A warm breeze came off the Atlantic, making the sheer white curtains billow, collapse, then fill with air again just like sails on a ship on a windy day. Each stream of sea air that came in whistled a different tune. A new day had dawned for Blake. He had looked forward to the research, hoping to find anything that might explain the mystery that had been set before him the night of July 13 when he slept on the beach—the night of his birthday.

That morning, on the way to The Maritime Library and Museum of Utter Ville, which was not big at all, nor far from home, Blake said to his father, "I've realized that I haven't heard the voices these past few days. Do you think they're gone?"

"Hum, really?" was the captain's only reply, then silence the rest of the way. He was often quiet when thinking—thinking why Blake was tormented some days and not others?

Upon entering through the library's thick, glass doors, Blake immediately smelled the sea, and saw that the shelves contained many books about the sea—the Marines, the Navy, and anything having to do with the ocean. Display cases exhibited small ship models from as far back as the 1500s, including the USS Constitution—but no sign of the Guerriere. As Blake raked the displays with his eyes, he observed military uniforms and weaponry from North America and Britain. Other displays embedded in walls had live colorful sea creatures, including an octopus, swimming in salt-water tanks. When Blake saw the octopus, he thought that sometimes his brain seemed surrounded by octopuses' tentacles, just squeezing until his brain would explode. There were sand tables, starfish, and shells for the public to touch. Blake went to the book section almost immediately. In awe, he turned to the captain. "Take a look at these three old books. They date back to the 1600s."

The captain reached for the books in Blake's hands. "Hum. Let me look at them." He leafed through the pages. "No. Nothing. Not in these books. They might be too old." The captain placed the books in a 'not wanted' pile so that the librarian could re-shelve them. "Keep searching, Blake. You're doing great. You might find an unusual link tied to the ship's mystery. Jot down every bit of information you find on the ship Guerriere, whether you are familiar with it or not. That will help narrow any thought or fact that you and I might have after we do the process of elimination—we'll rule out all common knowledge when we compare notes."

"How long do you think this will take?" Blake asked his father.

"It could take hours, days, weeks, months, even years. I hope that won't be the case here..." the captain paused, "...but, you must be patient."

"I know. I just want this whole thing to be over soon, that's all."

"I understand. So, do I. I get no pleasure in seeing you go through the ups and downs of hearing voices one day, and then the next you don't. My only wish is that it all stops—forever—if it's true." The last under his breath, but Blake heard his mumble.

"I'm afraid the voices will come back. I don't want to feel like an octopus has my brain wrapped up in its tentacles again."

The more Blake thought of the time he slept at the beach where it all began, Mr. DeMarcus' glass eye that didn't move, the stench at the coast guard station, the creepiness of hearing voices cry out his name, the more he felt his body pulsate. He stood motionless, looking intently at the captain, waiting for him to give some sort of response.

"Don't worry," said his father. "I'll help you as best as I can until this thing is over, even if it kills me. I promise."

Blake became uneasy. "But Dad, what if it never goes away?"

The captain swept his face with his hand, and then rested it over his mouth. Captain deWolfe turned away. "Blake, look at the reference section of the library while I stay here. See what you come up with, and then we will compare notes. How does that sound? Try focusing on any book that dates early-to-mid 1800s. That should narrow the search, I hope."

Blake felt a bit more at ease. "Great idea. But how long do you think it will take today?"

"It can take all day just to glance at the books, let alone to research them."

"Wow."

Blake walked over to the reference section with shelves holding hundreds of old books. The library was very old and had kept its antiquity. No modern technology—no computers in this library. *This search will take me my whole life.* He had to look through the card catalogs. He searched for hours.

Blake didn't realize how much time had elapsed until he looked at the ship's wheel clock on the sea-foam-green wall. "It's five o'clock already!" he said aloud. He gathered his things and walked over to where the captain was. "Dad, we've got to be leaving soon. Did you find anything?"

"I can't believe it. It feels like we just got here, and we've been here for eight hours? And no, nothing. I didn't find even a lead," said Captain deWolfe. The captain glanced at Blake while collecting his things.

Blake responded, "I know, I know what you're going to say: 'Be patient.' I'll try, Dad." The captain gave a half-smile at his son.

That night after supper, Blake went by the beach. Shortly after he arrived, the sky threatened to storm, and it became very windy. The restless voices spoke again.

"BLAKE, BLAKE, you must save us before the sun sets on August 19th."

"Why before the sun sets August 19th? What is the meaning of that date?" asked Blake.

The voices kept repeating *"Before the sun sets on August 19th,"* then faded away.

Blake felt driven by a force. A force that engulfed him; a force to search the mystery that was behind the Guerriere. Painstakingly, for twenty-four days, and for hours each day, he searched, and he still did not find one clue. The voices continued to disturb him every night.

On day 26 of the investigation, Blake walked over the card catalog index, pulled out the wooden drawer, and began to research all over again. He marked down some numbers that he thought might be useful. He walked over to the section but none of the books served his purpose. Tired and weary, he turned and glanced at the open shelves.

Suddenly, he saw a strange looking book that seemed to have popped out of nowhere. It had collected dust on a side shelf in the library. It had some sort of image on it. Blake's hands began to tremble as he reached for it. He took the book and blew off its dust, then wiped it with his hand to see the image. Blake's eyes widened. "The Guerriere!" he shouted. The people around him shushed him for being so loud. Blake immediately sat down with his notebook and pen to jot down as much as he could from the pages of that book. His journal entry went like this:

"Today is August 16th. I have been doing an intense study concerning a ship that an old sea captain named DeMarcus sold to my dad; but there seems to be some sort of secrecy attached somewhere. This is what I have found.

"The British HM Frigate Guerriere was in fact a French ship. It was captured, and then owned by the British Royal Naval Force. It did in fact fight with The Frigate of the United States Navy, The Constitution, an American ship, in the War of 1812.

The word 'frigate' means a warship that had anywhere from 28 to 60 guns on it, and the guns had been on two decks. It had a quarterdeck and forecastle along with other ship riggings. In my dream, I do remember all those guns sticking out of some small portholes, and I do remember all those guns on the deck.

"The weather was cloudy and windy. I wonder if the voices ride the wind? It appears that I only hear them when the northeast wind comes in heavy. Could it be? Because of the wind, the Guerriere was rolling in the mist of the mad, black sea. Her guns were under water, and she couldn't make her way up again.

"One of the biggest of sixteen warships the Americans had been The Constitution. The Constitutions side-walls were just short of two feet in thickness. Could that be why one of the British soldiers said it had the sides of iron in my dream?

"The Guerriere's gun breeching were all rotten and snapped like a twig. Many of their tackle bolts were loose and the guns couldn't be controlled properly. Although the ship itself looked in tip-top shape, it really wasn't. The Guerriere needed major repair. After the Guerriere's mast was shot and fell over, the ship couldn't function anymore. The American ship set it ablaze, and then it sank.

"Here's a piece of news: The battle took place 800 miles off the Grand Banks of Boston on August 19th! Is that why the voices are telling me they need to be freed by the evening of the 19th of August? That's the best clue, and that doesn't leave me much time.

Am I to rescue the spirits, on the same date and time, 200 years later? I must say that when I began to investigate the ship Guerriere, everything seemed bleak at first. I couldn't find anything. But the more I searched, the more I realized how strange it was to dream of being on a British ship during a heated battle with a man wearing a patch over his eye. Strangely enough, even the smell of rotting flesh that came over the ship, and the fire that came from nowhere, is making a bit more sense to me. Also, the voices that I've heard in the wind when no one else couldn't hear them. The strange Mr. DeMarcus too, although I don't have a full grasp yet of where DeMarcus fits in all this mess. Do I need to see him one more time? Yes! He will know the answer to the August 19th mystery. I know he will."

After he had completed his writings, Blake held out the black and white composition notebook to the captain. "Dad, read what I've found. I think we need to see Mr. DeMarcus one more time."

"Let's see." The captain opened the notebook and began to read. "Blake, you've done a terrific job on the bits and pieces you've found. But why do you want to see DeMarcus again?"

"Remember I told you that the voices said I have to free them before the evening of August 19th?"

"Yes."

"Well, the battle took place somewhere in the late afternoon on August 19th. What I don't get is that the voices kept telling me that they want to be freed by sunset. What is so important about the sun setting? I'll bet my life that DeMarcus knows the answer."

"Okay then, grab your things and let's go see him now." They hurriedly gathered their belongings, and out of the library they went. They darted into the captain's vehicle that was parked under the tall, whispering willow trees that kept the Hummer cool from the summer's sun. They kept silent all the way as they drove to The Coast Guard Station to meet with DeMarcus one more time.

Chapter 7: A Legend

Driving up the dusty driveway that led to The Coast Guard Station, Blake felt the silence break by the beating of his heart in his ears. He was so paralyzed with fear that he almost forgot the reason he wanted to see DeMarcus again, but knew he had to.

Captain deWolfe parked his vehicle in the dusty, graveled parking lot under a very old, half-dead oak tree and got out. "Are you coming, Blake?".

Blake trembled. "I'm coming." He sighed, and composed himself, getting out of the vehicle slowly, catching up to his father.

At a quick pace, they entered the broken-down shack. Captain deWolfe shouted, "Mr. DeMarcus! Are you in here?" There was no answer. The captain looked out a dirty window which led to the foggy pier and saw a silhouette of a slightly hunched man, dressed in British clothing, almost resembling the one that was in the Utter Ville's library in one of the display cases. "There he is, by the water. Why on God's earth is it always foggy around here? And I thought it was sunny out. The weather changed real fast," said the irritated captain.

"I was thinking that same thought, Dad."

Blake could hear the hollow *thump* of their shoes on the splintered, wooden pier as they went out to meet him. "Mr. DeMarcus, Blake found some information about the Guerriere over at The Maritime Library and Museum of Utter Ville, but we still have questions you might be able to answer."

"And what might they be?" answered DeMarcus in a high-pitched voice.

"Well, I was by the beach," said Blake, "and a northeast wind kicked up and the voices came back and said that I have to save them by sunset of August 19th. What exactly does it mean?"

Mr. DeMarcus peered into Blake's eyes. "Are ye willing to help them at any cost?"

"Well, yeah. Sure. I guess so." Blake swallowed hard.

"Well then, listen and do exactly what I say. It's the only way the voices will stop haunting ye. Ye understand me lad?"

Blake looked at his father. "Yeah, tell me what I have to do. Can my father help me when I go?"

"Yes, he can. But it's all up to ye, Blake. Ye were chosen because of yer bravery. I've watched ye for a very long time on these docks. Everyone talks about the young lad deWolfe. It's good, real, good. Yer honest. Ye've got zeal for life, and yer quick on yer feet, and a quick thinker, may I add. I know ye will do the job that is needed without hesitation."

"Well, thanks. That's very flattering coming from you," said Blake. For the very first time, Blake felt sorry for the old sea captain and felt the need to help him. Blake even felt himself beginning to like him.

DeMarcus repeated some things Blake already knew, and some things he wasn't sure about. "To answer yer question, in the evening of August 19th is when the Guerriere was so damaged, that poor vessel. It caught fire and sunk deep down into the dark Atlantic." DeMarcus paused, then continued, "The spirits on the Ghost Ship are restless because they want to be buried in their homeland. They want to rest in the place they were a part of before their bodies were destroyed by the vastness of the ocean, and the sea creatures eating away at them until they were nothing but bones. I vowed to help them, but being wounded meself in war—shot in the back that is—there wasn't much dat I could do. Derefore, I chose ye boy. Coincidental, one has your name. Yes, but I knew once I told ye dat, ye would search until ye found what ye needed to."

"You mean you tricked me?" Blake lunged at DeMarcus, about to tell him a few things, but then decided to hold his peace. He only said, "That wasn't very nice of you!"

"No lad. I just needed ye to act in the right way. Dat is all." Ha-ha-ha-he-he-he ha-whooo. Mr. DeMarcus began to laugh his awful laugh that so frightened Blake a few weeks ago.

Blake's eyes were fixed at the five-foot, dirty hunched old man, with matted hair, and a still green glass eye at half-mast. A gruesome sight he was. But his words somehow changed things. Blake no longer saw a decrepit old man, but one who needed his help. The captain's role would be guidance, moral and spiritual support, and of course, muscular power. "Mr. DeMarcus, tell me something. If the ship was destroyed as you and some of the history books claim, then how did you sell my dad a ship that looks like the Guerriere, or Ghost Ship as you put it?"

"*He-he-he-ha-ha.* Legend has it that the Guerriere was reconstructed by shadows; some people claim it to be the spirits of the thirteen dead still trapped in the ship way down under in the bottom of the sea. Every year on the 19th of August, in the night, the reconstruction took place until its completion." As the weathered face, dingy looking old man spoke, the sky opened, and a flash of light zoomed by. The cabin shook when the lightning split a nearby tree.

"Dear God of heaven and earth!" said the captain.

Blake's hairs on his arm stood straight up, but he didn't seem to care, so engrossed, almost hypnotized was he by what DeMarcus was saying. The crackling thunder and streaks of light flashing through the darkened sky were ignored. "I think we are ready..." Blake said to DeMarcus, and then looked at his father's reaction, "...right Dad?"

"Yes, I believe we are Blake; if we make it out of here alive with that electrical storm going on out there. We'll do whatever preparation is necessary tonight."

DeMarcus spoke again. "And ye have only two and a half days to rescue them from the ship, by 6:30 p.m. at sundown. Or ye would never be left alone. They will always haunt ye."

Blake swallowed hard at that threatening thought. He whispered frightfully, "Then what do I have to do?"

"Then ye have another task to do for the completion of setting the spirits free. Remember I told ye that they need to be buried in their homeland? Well after the nineteenth, within forty-eight hours of that time, ye need to bury them in British territory and dat will be the end of all yer troubles.

Blake was thinking, *why within forty-eight hours?*

Then DeMarcus, as if he had read Blake's mind, answered, "Because their bones will begin to deteriorate. Their bones have been preserved by the salt of the sea." Another bolt streaked by, and then ka-boom-boom-bom-bom went the rolling thunder.

"Good God in heaven. I don't know if I have enough time to do all this," said Blake in a panic.

"Ye must do as I say, or ye won't be freed from them. Ha-ha-ha-ha." Mr. DeMarcus turned and walked out the door when the lightening raced through the sky. Blake followed him out the door with his eyes, and he quickly disappeared into the storm.

That evening, Captain deWolfe, Blake, and Elizabeth packed salted pork that the captain had made a while ago; beef jerky, tea, coffee, sugar, powdered milk, loaves of homemade bread, dried fruit, marmalade, and huge flasks of fresh water. They also packed rope of all sizes, canvases, clothing, candles and kerosene from the candle shop that Sarah dropped off on her way home from work, and lastly a flashlight with some extra batteries. When all the packing was done, the three of them went down by the beach to relax a little.

Elizabeth pulled out from a burlap bag a Maritime Bible and handed it to the captain. "Here, take this…" she said in a gentle voice, "…remember how it helped you other times when trouble came your way at sea. Read it, both of you. God will give you comfort and strength when you need it. May God be with you."

The captain took the Bible from Elizabeth, kissed her, and then embraced her slender neck not wanting to let go; but found himself releasing her from his embrace. "Thank you. I love you. We will return. I promise you that." Then the captain let out a sigh.

Blake interrupted, "Dad, it looks like we have everything we need for this trip and set to go. Right?"

"Yes. We will leave first thing in the morning."

They all turned, and walked up the sixty-six, sun bleached steps toward home to get a good-nights rest for the big adventure that would lie ahead.

Chapter 8: The Voyage

Early the next morning the sky was orange-red. It stormed again. Blake and Captain deWolfe were by the docks ready to go, but were delayed because of torrential rain. "This has been such an unusual wet and hot August. I can't remember a time when the weather has been this crazy," said Blake's father. "I'm ready to call off this rescue project."

Blake reminded the captain that it had to be done by sunset of the nineteenth, and that the dead men's bones had to be buried within forty-eight hours after the initial rescue from the ship. He kept praying and hoping for the weather to clear, so they could begin their journey to the very spot where the Guerriere and the Constitution engaged in battle off the Grand Banks, near Boston.

"Dad, time is running out. I've calculated; it will take approximately thirty hours to reach the spot where the battle took place. If we face some trouble at sea, it will take longer. I think we are cutting this thing really close." Blake began to feel his stomach roll in circles.

"What time is it Blake?"

"Quarter to one. We've wasted so much time waiting for the weather to clear up, and it hasn't." Blake felt his face turn hot with anger toward the whole situation with the weather not cooperating. "Dad, we've got to chance it. We've got to go, now."

"Maybe you're right." Just then a little breeze blew by, and the rain calmed down with it. "Maybe when we're at sea we'll have more wind. If we're lucky, hopefully we can hoist the sails, and the rain will die off altogether."

Blake and the captain hauled the last items they needed onto the ship and boarded it. Off they went to sail what seemed to be an endless sea. After a short while, the rain clouds did burn off, and the sun shone brightly. There were more breezes, but nothing that could have helped speed up their sailing time. Captain deWolfe trusted Blake at the helm of the ship. Blake, steering into the horizon said, "Look at that fiery looking sunset. It's glowing red throughout the sky and in this great big ocean.

The waves' foam was red too." Blake left the helm and went over to the ship's quarterdeck to get a better view of the vastness of the red horizon and the red sea that had no end.

Captain deWolfe went quickly to fetch some of the provisions they carried on board. They sat down on deck to eat some homemade bread, beef jerky, tea, and coffee for supper while watching the extraordinary sunset. Unbelievingly, the first few hours were smooth sailing.

That night, before turning in, the captain opened the Maritime Bible. Out loud, he read the first thing his finger touched, "Fear not, for I am with you; be not dismayed, for I am your God. I will strengthen you, Yes, I will help you, and I will uphold you with my righteous right hand. That's Isaiah 41:10."

"Dad, one of my tee-shirts has *Do Not Fear* on it. It reminds me of that scripture you just read. When I was scared the other day, those words did bring me comfort. Maybe mom is right after all. The more you read the Bible, the more comfort it brings you."

Captain deWolfe patted Blake on the back. "I'll drop anchor here, so we can settle and turn in when we want to. Who knows what tomorrow will bring? But I do know that we need our rest for tonight."

"Is it okay if I sleep out on the deck tonight?"

"Sure. The sky cleared up pretty good. That's something we haven't seen too much of this August. I can't believe how it cleared so quickly either. I thought we were going to have rain all day. And the stars came out, which makes it a beautiful night."

Blake set out a portable cot with a blanket out on deck, still eating some bread from his supper. The night air soothed him. As he watched the bright stars twinkle in the black velvety sky, he quickly dozed off. He slept all night peacefully.

That next morning the dawn was misty. The ship rocked. A warm south wind blew, but he slept on. Suddenly he awoke to the strong sound of flapping wings. "What was that?" He saw a seagull flying over him, trying to peck at the bread he still held from last night's supper. "You, stu-

pid bird. What are you doing all the way out here? I guess you've lost your way. Well you scared me, dummy!" Blake threw the piece of bread overboard to rid himself of the annoying gull. It made him feel uneasy. It reminded him of the night where it all began, the night he slept on the beach; the night when he heard the voices torture him to the point of questioning his own sanity.

The previous night's biblical reading of, 'Not Being Afraid' temporarily left Blake. Then, he felt fear creep over him again. It covered him like an un-welcomed blanket on a summer's night. He was fearful of the voices coming back to irk his mind; fear of the unknown at sea traveling ahead toward the spot to rescue the bones of the spirits that haunted him. And fear of not returning home—ever!

Chapter 9: Ghost Ship

The day grew hotter. The sun beat down on Blake and the captain. Blake, to protect his skin from burning more, put on a long-sleeved, blue-jean shirt, soaked in sea water. "I can't believe it. Today is the 19th of August, and it's getting late. We don't see any signs of the battle of the USS Constitution and the Guerriere," said Blake. An hour later, the wind had stopped. The air was as still as a corpse. Blake's auburn hair damp from sweat drooped over his face. He still felt the heat penetrate his skin. "There is no breeze at all for these sails. What do we do?" Blake paced the floor and ran his nervous hands through his face and head.

"We sit and wait. That is all we can do for now, and hope to God we make it on time."

They drifted along in the enormous glass-like sea. Suddenly, Blake pointed toward the sky. "Look Dad. There is strange lighting. It looks like the sea and the sky are connected."

Before long, they had no choice but to follow its path. "I think the light has some sort of magnetic pull on this ship," said Blake nervously.

Captain deWolfe gripped the ship's tiller. "Full speed ahead!" he shouted, but the rudder would not turn. The sea grew extremely rough, water vigorously slapping the sides of the frigate. The sea rushed toward them, and the ship jumped the turbulent waves.

Blake pointed in the direction of the strange light again, "A ghost ship, Dad!" The wind blew hard in his face. He was excited but frightened at the same time. Their ship was being sucked closer and closer, faster and faster, slicing through the dark cold waters like it had a mind of its own. "Dad, take out your map of sea battles. Check your compass to see if this is the same place where the Americans and the British engaged, and if this is where the Guerriere sank."

Soon they were fifty yards from the Ghost Ship. Blake's eyes widened. "That ship looks exactly like ours. Only that one looks ragged, torn and abandoned."

When they were twenty-five yards away, the force stopped. The captain was able to steer his ship against the wind. "What time is it, Blake?"

Blake looked at his watch. "Oh, my goodness. It is quarter to six. We will have to get on that ship and find the bones before sunset. We don't have much time!" exclaimed Blake. Blake looked up at the captain, concerned with perplexed eyes. "Dad, why are you going the wrong way?" He went into a panic, throwing his hands as he spoke. "We have to get close enough, so I can jump on her deck, and you are making the wrong turns. We've got to get on board that ship!"

Captain deWolfe shouted, "Where is the ship?!"

Blake gasped for air, shook his head, and pointed toward it. "It's about thirty yards south of where we are now. The wind is starting to pick up, fast."

"*B-L-A-K-E, B-L-A-K-E, SAVE US B-L-A-K-E.*"

"Oh no, the voices are back." Blake covered his ears.

"Are you sure you're hearing the voices you heard at the beach?"

"I'm dead sure," said Blake. "Only this was much louder and echoed in my ears. Dad, can't you hear them?"

"No. I don't. And I don't know why."

"*B-L-A-K-E, HELP US,*" the voices continued.

Blake pressed harder on his ears, gritting his teeth. "Dad, make them stop!"

"*B-L-A-K-E, B-L-A-K-E. Come quickly B-L-A-K-E-!*" screamed the voices in a screeching high pitch, that could burst any-persons eardrum.

"All right already, I'm coming!" He shouted back at the incredible turbulent wind. "Dad, we need to get onto that ship." Blake, though weary, was determined to rescue the bones of the restless spirits that troubled him. The waves through droplets of murky sea water into his eyes, blowing with more force as every minute passed. Captain deWolfe and Blake fought to stand on their feet.

"It's too dangerous, but we must risk going on board." Blake paid no mind to his soaked hair and clothing. He didn't care about sliding on the wet deck. He was determined to save the dead men's bones. By now, the ships were close enough to jump, "Dad, throw the rope ladder over to the other ship!" he shouted pointing in The Ghost Ship's direction.

They fought the heavy winds and dense fog for almost half an hour; it seemed like forever. Blake pointed to the direction of the ship again. Captain deWolfe's arms bulged when he picked up the thick-knotted rope and threw it across to The Ghost Ship. The sea spit its black waters into their ship. An inch of water on the deck made it even more treacherous. Captain deWolfe pulled on the rungs and pulled himself up and over the side, over the strange fierce water. "I'm going across Blake!" the captain cried. The wind pushed his long, wet hair in every direction.

Blake knew his father couldn't see the other ship. "Dad, be careful!" The captain began to slither on his belly across the ladder. His stained, white, cotton shirt filled with air and puffed out like the curtains in Blake's bedroom. Halfway across, a strong gust of wind blew, shaking the ladder.

SPLASH!

"N-o-o Dad! Where are you? Blake cried, fighting to pull up the other side of the rope. "Dad, you have to show yourself, you have to be there, you have to be alive! You promised Mom that we were going to get home alive! I heard you tell her Dad. D-A-D!!!"

Blake's eyes filled with tears. He shook, became paralyzed, and then came quickly to his senses. *I mustn't panic. I can't lose hope now.* Blake continued to fight with the rope, trying to untangle it while pulling it up. "Oh God, please help me. Give me the strength I need to save my dad." Blake abandoned the tangled rope for a moment, fell on his knees on the ships watery deck, and clasped his hands like his mother taught him to do in church every Sunday morning. "Please, God. I need his help to bury those dead men's bones who are on that ship, and Mom needs us both. Dad promised Mom that we would return back home."

Wiping his tears away with his hands, Blake got up, and continued to pull. His forearms bulged with a surge of energy that pumped into them, into him, into his whole body. His eyes searched the sea frantically. After a moment, he saw a distressed hand reach up from the murky water on one side of the thick twine ladder. Blake thought quickly and tied the already loosened rung onto one of the ship's rigging supports where they stored cord. Pushing against the wind, his clothes slapped loudly as they jerked; he swung his leg over the twine ladder and was on his way down. The wind, strong and wild, threatened to knock him into the greenish brown, dirty-foamed, raging sea. Blake had reached the last rung when the wind succeeded and knocked him into its swirling mouth.

"*B-L-A-K-E, WE N-E-E-D YOU, WE N-E-E-D YOU NOW. HELP US B-L-A-K-E!*"

Blake looked at the enormous, mad sea. His head bobbed in and out of the water, making him gasp for air. His clothes weighed him down. Blake loosened the buttons from his jean shirt, took it off, and let it fall into the sea. He moved swiftly in taking off his sneakers too. Feeling a bit lighter he answered the voices, "I'm here! I'm trying to save my own father! You're going to have to wait, you, stupid voices. I've had enough of your torment! My Dad comes first. Are you hearing me? My Dad comes first!"

He turned around and spotted the captain's head, and then swam under where his foot was trapped by the roping of the ladder. Blake quickly emptied his zippered, nylon shorts pocket of a small pocketknife he always carried and cut his father loose. Grabbing the captain by the hair, he pulled him up over one of the rungs of the rope ladder, hoping that he was breathing. "N-o-o! Don't go. You can't leave me to do this all by myself. Please come back. I need you."

Blake pounded and wept on his father's back. "God please, bring him back to me." He suddenly felt a weakness overtake him, his emotions. He cried out, "And help me get him up this ladder." Blake wiped his tears and nose with his shaking hands. He managed to pick up his father, and carried him over his shoulder, up the rungs. When he reached the top, they tumbled onto the ship's deck. "Dad," Blake panted, rolling him onto his back and tilting his unshaven chin to open his airway. He pinched the captain's nose with an unsteady hand, took a deep breath, and then breathed into the captain's mouth over, and over again.

His dad's chest rose, and the air escaped from his nose with a weak hiss, but he wouldn't breathe on his own. "Dad, I can't do this. I will have to get those bones off that ship or we'll both die. D-a-d!" Blake pounded on his father's chest. There was still no response. Cradling his father's head in his arm he slapped his face, appalled at his own actions. He stared at his father's wet, cold flesh, still hoping, "Dad!" he screamed again as he dropped his father's head and got to his feet. Running his hands through his soaked hair, he left his father lying lifeless in a puddle and ran to the rail, searching for a way onto The Ghost Ship.

Blake could see that the two ships where very close by now. He heard wood snap, and crash onto the deck behind him. He turned and saw it was the tip of one of the masts, and other pieces ready to fall. He ran and hid below deck until it was over. The ship swayed with the falling segments. When all was clear, Blake crawled out, peering around corners. He saw that a mast that had snapped off The Ghost Ship connected the two ships. *Perhaps a provision from God*, he thought. Blake examined the broken stump for a minute, and then jumped on. He hugged the stump with his arms and legs.

On his belly, he inched slowly across the bridge formed by the fallen mast. He made it onto The Ghost Ship despite the heavy wind and the feeling of helplessness.

He staggered to his feet on The Ghost Ship's deck. "This ship is creaking. The floorboards are loose. I'm afraid I might fall through the deck," Blake said aloud, as if his father was with him. Then Blake remembered the words of the captain: On an old ship, step on the creases between the floor planks, because they're nailed in. That's where the floor is most secure. Blake took his father's advice and, walking between the planks, entered the captain's cabin. He found nothing significant, but strangely enough, a glimpse of light shone through the porthole-like window. Something shiny sat on the captain's top bunk that caught Blake's eye. He slowly walked over to it. It was a shiny brass button. Blake put it into his wet shorts pocket and zippered it up.

"*B-L-A-K-E WE NEED YOU N-O-W BEFORE I-T-'S TOO L-A-T-E!*" howled the voices.

"I know! I'm on the ship. I'm trying to find you! Where are you?" Blake's voice was lost in the wind. He frantically searched the entire quarterdeck. Nothing. If this is called a Ghost Ship, Blake thought, Perhaps the bodies were dragged into the dungeon—in the brig of this ship. He said aloud, "That would make sense." He looked at his nautical watch, six-fifteen. "My God, help me. I have only fifteen minutes to rescue these bones so this torment in my life will be broken, hopefully for good."

The Ghost Ship was deteriorating. It was rotten, and the huge waves made matters worse by pulverizing the sides of the ship. The sounds of crashing, snapping wood filled the air. The foremast was so weak it cracked and toppled toward the mainmast and crows-nest, knocking it down, too. The tattered sails folded and plunged into the sea still tied to their masts. Blake heard the wood snapping behind him, then *CRASH*. The mizzenmast snapped off and bored a hole through the ship's deck. Blake quickly and carefully went down the steps, which led to the lower part of the ship, holding on to whatever he could to keep from falling. The only light source came from the huge hole where the mizzenmast had just crashed through, right into the brig. The ray of dull light shined directly on greenish, tarnished, brass nameplates, some dangling on one rusty screw, yet others on top of the bony victims. Blake's throat fluttered. His heart beat out of rhythm. His hands shook. His body felt limp. He was horrified at the sight of his name above one of the dead. *This place looks like some sort of a burying ground already.* Blake knew what he had come to do, but his imagination interrupted his focus, and it started to work against him. *Am I next? What if I never get out of here alive?*

Blake quickly shook his head and dismissed the question of him becoming the next victim and looked toward the skeletons. Blake spoke to them as if they were living, "No. I'm not going to let my thoughts get in my way. I have to find something to put each of you in.' He looked around. There were cobwebs everywhere. Shoving them aside in disgust, he made a doorway. At least fifty barrels sat on one side of the ship's storage area, across from the brig. In the barrels were all sorts of tools, ropes, canvases, even barrels of thick black tar. Blake knocked over the last barrel with his bare foot. It held some burlap bags. Okay, he thought. All I need is thirteen of them. He quickly counted thirteen and ran them over to where the skeletons lay. The ship rocked back and forth from the forceful wind. Blake slipped, fell, got up, then slipped again. He battled to stay on his feet. Drip, drip, drip. He heard water seeping into the lower deck near to where he was. Finally, he made his way back to the skeletons. Hurriedly, he grabbed the gruesome bones of one, and put his skeleton with his nameplate in the bag, then tied a knot so that nothing could escape. He continued until he was done. Blake frantically dragged two bags at a time onto the dilapidated ship's quarter deck until they were all together.

Then he shouted into the wind. "Dad, I'm doing this for you, for me, for Mom and for Mr. DeMarcus! This is all I can do. I was chosen to do this; so, spirits, if I die, you will never, I repeat, you will never have a resting place. Do you hear me, spirits? You never will unless I set you free!"

Streaks of lightning cut through the sky, hitting a small island in the middle of the sea, then *ka-booom, boom, bom* went the thunder. Blake looked in the direction of his father's ship and saw the streaks silhouette a shadow in the fog that encircled the two ships. A flashing thought crossed Blake's mind. *Could it be Dad? Alive?* Blake had to jump ship with the thirteen bags of bones before the ship went under. "I'm ready Dad! I'm doing this for you, for me, for Mom, and for Mr. DeMarcus! Don't know if I'll live or die, but all I do know is that I'll die trying if it must be!" Blake then took one bag at a time and threw it over until all thirteen bags were on board the Guerriere. The Ghost Ship creaked, cracked, and tilted to one side. It began to take on water.

Blake hurriedly made his way, pushing and shoving the debris and the wet, tattered sails and roping out of his way to make it to the mainmast that was still connected by the bow of the captain's ship. *CRACK, SMASH, Ka-b-o-o-o-m*, went part of the abandoned ship's side.

The Ghost Ship is rotting. I've got to make it across. Blake was drenched with sea water, and the constant rocking of The Ghost Ship made it hard to stand erect. There was a spooky, vicious dark cloud that encircled it too. The mad sea kicked its water so high that the frigate filled up to Blake's knees with the murky water. Around the other ship, there was a lighter cloud, or something like that, that encircled it. Somehow that one didn't seem so spooky.

Chapter 10: Dead Men's Bones

The waves were monstrous. Blake, worn out, managed to get on the wet, round mast that resembled a bark-less log, and slid his way back onto the Guerriere. He was almost at the end when he heard a loud rumble, cracking, screeching noise, and smelled smoke. Blake looked straight ahead, moving swiftly toward his mark. *Don't look back*, he warned himself. The long stump shifted as he jumped off then, *CRASH*, into the sea it went.

When he reached his father's ship, he looked back one time. The Ghost Ship was on fire, and the tip of its hull was going down, hopefully forever. Blake stood watching in awe, realizing he'd barely made it off that sinking, fiery ship.

Blake turned back to his father. The captain's body was missing from the deck. "Dad! Where are you?" he shouted. Blake felt his stomach cave in, and it was not from seasickness. Blake never got seasick. He had been at sea since he was born, when his mom would hold him in her arms in the cabin while Captain deWolfe steered the vessel they had called 'All Boy,' referring to Blake. Maybe the waves had tilted the ship enough to throw Dad overboard. "Dad, are you washed away at sea?' he asked, looking into the foamy waves, and not able to catch a breath. The floodgates of his eyes opened, and the rivers flowed down his cheeks, down his neck adding to his already wet chest. Blake moaned from the pain he felt inside. But, despite how he felt, Blake had a job to complete. He went to the burlap bags holding the bones of the British soldiers. His eyes widened in horror. The bags were missing too. Blake's imagination began to churn. Maybe some force had transferred Dad's body and bags onto the crow's nest. After all, a magnetic force sped up Dad's ship to reach the spot where the battle took place. Blake waited a minute to clear his mind, and then he went to search the ship. He began by looking up at the crow's nest to see if there was anything unusual. He climbed the turbulent rope rungs of the mainmast slowly and carefully to get a better look in the heavy wind. The ship was still swaying side to side, riding the waves.

"There is nothing up here, and I can't see anything down there," he said aloud, swallowing his words as the wind increased its force. Blake had a great and scary view from where he was. Holding onto one rope, for a split second, he noticed a silhouette of a hunched, disfigured man, woman, or beast.

Blake's imagination grew wild again. It reminded him of a nightmare he once had. There had been nothing but darkness where ever he turned. He heard the thumps of what he perceived to be that of a human heart. But whose heart? It got louder and louder. Blake dreamt he was running, running from what he did not know. Then he saw something in dim light, far off. Standing in front of him was a shadowy disfigured semi-human. Right before the hideous man, woman, or beast was revealed; he woke up in a sweat with his own heart beating untamed. Blake's body shook in fear remembering that revolting nightmare.

Then, *"B-L-A-K-E, B-L-A-K-E, HELP US B-L-A-K-E,"* called the voices again. Blake shouted into the wind, "What in God's creation do you want from me? I rescued you! I almost lost my own life in helping all of you!" Blake threw up his hands. "Oh, what does it matter to you anyway? You are all dead, but I'm still alive, ALIVE! And my dad, the captain of this ship, is missing, dead, I think."

Blake wiped the tears from his eyes, and then began to climb down the crow's nest. Blake, his eyes still watery, searched all around to see if he could see anything else, any clue to find his father and the dead men's bones. But he did not see anything else.

Blake staggered to the captain's cabin. He pushed open the rusty door and searched the bunks. Nothing. Not one soul. Not one bag of the sailor's bones. How can dad's body just disappear? And how can thirteen burlap bags of dead men's bones be gone too? There is something I'm missing, I just don't get it.

Exhausted, Blake lay down. Suddenly he felt the ship race, cutting through the sea with lightning speed. He quickly left the cabin and went over to the helm of the ship. But no one was at the helm. The Guerriere had a mind of its own once again, only this time, the magnetic force was pushing the ship *away* from the battle site. Blake could do nothing but sit on the wet deck, staring into nothingness and wait for it to stop.

An hour later, Blake realized the ship was slowing down. He got up slowly to stretch his cramped muscles. The storm was almost over too. Grim-faced, he hopped to the stairway which led to the galley of the ship to get a bite to eat. He thought a bite of beef jerky, salted pork and some bread would do him some good.

Everyone, including Dad, loved the ship's galley, he thought. Moving down the creaking steps, he heard something heavy breathing that did not sound human. He tiptoed back up the stairs, into the captain's cabin and reached for a flashlight. There he found the key to unlock a trap door and pulled out an emergency gun the captain had locked away in one of the splintered floorboards. Blake's hand was pierced through with a huge splinter as he moved the board. He quickly pulled it out and sucked the crimson liquid enough for it not to drip so much. Nervously holding the weapon, he carefully made his way back to the stairwell. He placed his feet, one by one, on the steps again, until he reached the bottom. Still tiptoeing, he turned the corner opposite the steps. The breathing grew louder and louder. Blake's heart began to beat hard. He felt the blood drain out of his face. Courageously, he shone the flashlight and pointed the gun in the direction of the nauseating clamor, not knowing what hellish thing he would find.

Blake gasped for air and turned on the flashlight. "Dad? Oh Dad. What on earth happened to you? How did you manage to get down here?" Blake dropped everything he had in his hands, ran up to the captain, and hugged his neck not waiting for an answer. "I thought you were some sort of creature lurking about. I thought I heard these weird sounds coming from the galley, but when I came down, it was coming from behind the steps, across from the galley and here you are. ALIVE!"

"My head and chest still hurt from all that water," spoke the captain in a slur, still feeling drowsy, holding his head tight.

"That's why you sound horrible. But how did you become conscious again?"

"I'm not sure. What I do know is that I woke up and felt myself in a puddle."

"Dad, I'm just glad to see you alive. I tried reviving you, but I didn't see you breathing. Time was running out, so I jumped ship to get the skeletons. I threw them over to this ship, but I can't find them anywhere."

The captain shook his head to wake up a bit more and got to his feet. "Blake, come with me." The captain asked, but barely could stand, or speak.

"Dad, don't get up. Rest a while."

"No. I'll be all right. I'm shaky, but still can move. Captain deWolfe went over to some storage barrels that were in the brig. "Open those five barrels."

"Are you hungry for something?" Blake could not figure out what the captain was up to. He found a flat piece of iron near the barrels and quickly pried them opened.

"The burlap bags! Dad, where did you find them?"

"Blake, let me explain something to you. You were given a special job to do, and you've done it. You were so engrossed in what you had to do that you were the only one who saw The Ghost Ship, or shall I say, was privileged to see it. I could not see the ship. Not even once. Just like DeMarcus said, you had to be the one to do the rescue, not me. However, as you flung the bags over, I was catching them. On this ship, the bags became visible to me. I saw them hurl through the sky and knew how important it was for you, for your sanity. No matter if they were empty or full, I was going to catch each one as if it was real to me as it is to you. When I caught each bag, I could feel what I assumed to be bones. Because I believe in you and what you were doing; when I peeked in a bag, I did see human bones with a tarnished nameplate. Therefore, I tied each one tight with cord I found in a barrel of supplies and placed them in some empty barrels and shut them securely in case the ship capsized in the extreme wind. This is what we came for and risked our lives, is it not?"

"Dad, you mean to tell me—oh my goodness! You were the one I saw from the mainmast crow's nest. I saw a disfigured thing that looked hunched back. Why did you look that way?"

"Probably because my shirt filled with air, and I was hunched over in pain."

"It makes sense," Blake said softly that the captain couldn't make out the words.

"Now let me finish," the captain continued in his weakness, "I carried three of them at a time in fear of this vessel turning over. I wanted to get them in a secure place as soon as possible."

"Dad, thank you so much in believing in me and helping me out. You almost lost your own life because of me." Blake was beaten from the day's event and yawned heavily. "It's almost nine o'clock, and I'm extremely tired. I know you must be too. Let's drop anchor here." As tired as Blake and his father were, Blake, before he turned in for the night, told the captain everything that had taken place on The Ghost Ship.

Chapter 11: Sickness Strikes

After Blake and Captain deWolfe talked about the rescue of what were once living British soldiers, Blake said, "I feel proud to be the one who was assigned to rescue those guys. But, the job's only halfway done. Mr. DeMarcus said that I have a couple of days to get these bones buried in British territory." Blake's moment of pride crumbled. He knew his geography, and they were nowhere near any such land.

"Only by the grace of God will we make it in time to bury them," replied the captain. "I have confidence in you, son. You've made it this far, and I'm sure if anyone can do it; it would be you. You can, and you will do what is commanded of you." Blake's determination began to rise at the inspiration of his father's words.

"I hope you're right, Dad."

Suddenly, a roar of wind catapulted the Gurriere westward. The ship hit turbulent weather as if some force was pulling them into the blackness of the sea, kicking up murky sea water, creating huge waves once again. Blake and his father fell hard on their back side, onto the deck. The bronze kerosene lamp went flying, shooting red-orange flames in every direction, but thankfully the heavy winds blew out the fire before it got out of hand. Rolling on the ship's floor, Blake and Captain deWolfe were tossed from one end of the ship to the other, and then smashed into the door of the captain's quarters. Thick clouds covered the moon, and the blackness of the sea increased the uncertainty of where they were headed.

Unable to see, Blake shouted, "What's happening?"

"I don't know," bellowed back the captain.

"What do you suppose is going on? Why is this happening again? Only this time it seems to be pulling us away from the battle scene." Blake sighed.

"I can only guess that in these waters there is some sort of a gravity, a magnetic pull that this ship is subject to. This never happened to any of the other ships I've sailed on in these parts of the sea before." The sea kept spitting its water onto the ship, as the waves pounced against its side.

"My suggestion is that we hold on for the ride. It has to come to a halt like before."

Concerned, Blake spoke, "Dad, the water is rising on deck. We need to get this water out of here before the ship overloads and sinks. Where are the buckets?"

"If you can make your way to the galley, there are some old, five-gallon wooden pickle barrels in one of the cabinets, under where the cutting boards are. Bring them up, and I'll try to make my way to the wheel to steady this vessel, that is, if it will let me."

Blake, got up slowly and began to walk, holding on to whatever he could to balance himself in the dim light. A thought came to him of when he was in one of his science classes. In class, the study was how eyesight works. The students pretended to be blind, and the teacher advised them to take smaller steps, depend on sound, and use their hands to feel their way through the classroom. Blake now was able to quickly use what he learned and felt his way to the galley. "I know, in one of the drawers there is a flashlight," he mumbled to himself. "I hope I can find it." Groping around the galley for several minutes, he found the drawer he thought it was in; pulled it open, stuck one hand in the draw and fumbled around until he felt the shape of the precious, metal object. In a state of relief, "I found it! Yes, I found it!"

He grabbed it, switched the "on" button, shone the light around the galley and found the spot the captain was talking about. Holding onto the wall, still to keep balanced, he took small steps to reach the seemingly distant cabinet. He moved the wooden fastener and peered into the black hole, then shone the light inside. "Oh no. There are no pickle barrels here. What do I do. Think-think-think!" Blake exclaimed. He then closed his eyes and held his head tightly, not letting go of the flashlight. Let me think a minute. I've got to find something to get the water out. Blake began to look around slowly. The water is starting to seep through the boards down here. I've got to find something in a hurry. Blake lost his footing and flew head first into some old storage shelves. Without giving it much thought, he quickly got up on his feet again. I know. I'll go where the bigger barrels are to see if there might be something I can bring up. He then made his way to the brig, which had been used for storage. He shone the light to exam it. In disappointment, There are no smaller barrels here. Now what? Blake held his stomach. I feel like I'm about to get sick, he said to himself, then held his head. The room spun. "I'm soo-soo-dizz...." Blake collapsed between two huge wooden ribs on the floor, hitting his head on one of them.

Not knowing what had happened, Blake opened his eyes slowly to the captain coddling his neck, pushing his clumped hair from his face, and gently tapping a gash on his forehead, keeping the blood from running into his eyes. Feeling weak, "Dad. You've found me. I was looking for the barrels just as you asked me too, then suddenly, I felt woozy Dad, I was getting seasick. But, I never get seasick. I think I was so stressed that I passed out."

"How are you feeling now?" the captain asked.

"Not so good. I have the chills."

"Maybe you're coming down with something. Let me feel your head. Hum, you do feel very warm. I hope you can ride it out until we bury these skeletons in British territory."

"Dad. What about the ship? Is there a lot of water on deck? Are we going to sink? Are we going to die?"

The captain rubbed Blake's brow, "Shhh. I think you need to lie down awhile."

"No, Dad. I'm going to help you," Blake responded fighting his way up.

The captain pushed Blake back down gently, "You need to rest. You'll need your energy for digging."

Drip, drip, drip. Blake could hear and see the water seeping through the crakes of the ship's floorboards. The wooden ribs in the hold below deck were filling too. The captain picked up Blake's wet body, brought him into the galley, laid him in a huge hole on the side of the wall, with a cutting board sticking out directly over it. "Here. You'll fit in this large cabinet. I'll find some burlap to cover you for now. You'll be safe and warm in here. I'll come back for you when this freakish magnetic force lets go of us."

Blake couldn't help but to notice the fear in his father's eyes as he spoke. The captain looked at Blake, patted his bloodied forehead one last time, got up, and grabbed some pots Elizabeth had left on hooks by the small portable gas stove. "This isn't much, but it's something." Hurriedly, the captain turned, and up the steps two by two he went to try to save the ship and their very lives.

When the captain left the galley, Blake threw off the burlap bags that served as a blanket. He twisted his way out of the splintering wooden cabinet, took the flashlight with his unsteady hand, and shined it recklessly. He looked up and saw, nailed to the wall, other pots hanging. In his weak state, he managed to climb up and get two of them down. Then Blake staggered up the steps to help Captain deWolfe bail-out sea water from the ship's deck. "What are you doing here? I told you to rest."

"No, Dad. If you're out here bailing water, then so am I. I can't let you do this all by yourself."

"But you're not well and you're running a fever. You'll need your strength later."

Blake sternly stared into the captain's eyes. "If I don't help bail this water out, there might not be a-later-on, Dad. If this ship sinks, we're dead, but I won't die from using my muscles to bail out water from this vessel with a fever, and a gash on my head."

The captain gave up, smiled at Blake, then patted him on his back saying, "Okay then. Try to brace yourself as best as you can and start bailing out the water, sailor."

Blake stood tall when his father called him "sailor". He gave the captain a crooked smile and went to work. "Thanks for letting me, Dad," said Blake feeling proud.

After ten minutes, the ship slowed down. The sea stopped spewing its black waters onto the ship's deck. Oddly, Blake realized that the storm quickly cleared. There was never a compromise in the weather these days. When there was a storm, it quickly cleared up. If nice, suddenly the weather turned crappy. Even though, when Blake looked at the sky, hope filled his heart. He saw the haze of the Milky Way so beautifully formed. He saw the planets show off their brilliant shine. He saw millions of bright stars twinkling like shining diamonds against the velvety black sky. He saw the shooting stars show off their glowing streaks once again.

Chapter 12: Map

After the storm cleared, there was very little water left on the deck, because Blake and the captain worked endlessly to bail out as much water possible not to sink. By the dim light of kerosene lanterns, they also pulled up the mainmast canvas without trouble. It was now easy sailing. The night was slightly breezy and warm.

The captain turned to Blake, "How are you feeling, and do you still feel very warm?"

"I feel beaten up from being tossed around. I can't believe how the wind was blowing, and how the waves were smashing into the ship. Other than that, I don't feel sick or feverish anymore."

"Wow! Your fever broke in record time."

"Yeah, it does seem quite odd. Why do you suppose I was sick for such a short time?"

"Maybe that freaky force had something to do with it," stated the captain in unbelief.

"Dad, you might have a very good point. It makes total sense. I was the one who went onto The Ghost Ship to rescue the thirteen skeletons. It seemed like that force or forces were fighting to keep me from making it to British soil to bury them. What else could it be?" Blake paused, then continued. "Dad, were you aware of the ship slowing down after I came up to help you? Did you notice how the storm cleared up and the stars suddenly appeared so brightly without a cloud in the sky? It seems once I made the choice to do something right, this eerie evil broke that was upon us. Could it be so?" questioned Blake still uncertain of it all.

"Come on Blake. It might come as a disappointment to you, but I was not serious about connecting the force with how you felt." The captain tapped his temple with his finger as he usually did when becoming suspicious of anything, then he spoke, "But then again, perhaps you are right. It could not all be a coincidence.".

Blake, hoping for a logical reply asked his father, "Do you think the gravity pull, the voices I've heard, being sick for a very short time, and all this diabolical madness will happen again?"

"I don't know. I cannot answer that, Blake. Why did you hear voices and I didn't? Why did you see the ship, and I only pretended to? Why did you have a fever and passed out, and then have a miraculous comeback? Who knows, maybe we will never have answers. But one good thing that came out of that force pulling us, we will be docking in Greenville Seaport in record time."

Blake cringed. "Oh Dad, why do I feel so scared all over again? I thought once I rescued the thirteen skeletons I'd be okay. I don't feel okay at all," he said feeling a cold chill crawling up and down his spine.

"Blake, you're feeling anxious because I've mentioned docking at Greenville Seaport. I know you've had some bad experiences there, but I'm with you now. That's all. You'll be fine. Remember, I'm here with you. You are not alone," said the captain with reassuring words, trying to comfort his son.

Blake, holding his stomach, "So then, when are we docking?"

"In an hour or so."

"I wish that I could rest my head on a pillow, but I feel so restless."

Steering the ship, the captain turned to Blake, "That's a great idea. Why don't you head over to the captain's cabin, and try putting your head on the pillow?"

Blake knew he couldn't close his eyes. "I'll go read something instead." Blake loved to read. He took one of the lit kerosene lanterns and walked over to the captain's quarters. He pushed the squeaky hinged wooden door open and saw that there was a small shiny object on the floor. He put the lantern on a hook on the wall, then turned to pick up the shiny object. "Where did it go?" he said to himself. Blake searched the cabin's deck but could not find what he saw when he first entered the room. "I know I saw something gleaming." Blake searched through his short's pocket that was on the bed for the gold button he had found on board The Ghost Ship. *Hmm. I didn't open this zipper, and there are no holes. How can it be gone?* he thought, shrugging his shoulders. He threw the shorts back onto the bunk, picked up the lantern from its hook, left the room, and went toward the helm of the ship. But, before he left the captain's quarters, he scanned the room with his eyes one last time for that puzzling gleaming object.

"Blake, if you don't mind, come steer since you're not resting. It might help you get your mind off all that has happened."

Blake's feet squished inside his last pair of sneakers as he walked. "Dad, it is totally amazing on how we bailed most of the water out using Mom's pots." Blake paused. "I miss Mom," he said softly.

"Yes. I miss her too," said the captain sympathetically. "And you are right," he continued shifting emotions, "When you said it was amazing how we bailed out water using Mom's pots. Oh boy, only if she knew." The captain chuckled. "Mom's pots saved our lives. The deck still has some sea water, but not enough to sink this ship," he said with a half a smile.

An hour passed, and Blake was still at the helm. "I can see the light shining from the old lighthouse, Dad."

"Another few minutes and we will be pulling up to the ol' dock," said the captain.

The ship drifted toward the fat pilings, which stood at attention, guiding and welcoming the incoming vessels. "We're here. We've made it," Blake sighed with relief.

"Okay, steer her in steady," said the captain motioning with his hands in which direction to turn while eyeing the dock.

As Blake took his father's cues, and was coming in slowly to dock the Guerriere, a dense fog crept around them once again like an octopus engulfing its prey. Screech, squeak, thump. "I hit one of the pilings." "Throw the rope over and try to catch one of the hooks."

Blake threw the rope but could not reach the hook. "How about if I catch one of the pilings? They are a lot bigger and I can spot them better."

"Try it." The captain grabbed the rope and tied a huge noose then handed it back to Blake, "Here Blake. Steady your hands and go for it."

Blake threw the rope and caught the piling on the first try. "What luck! Did you see that Dad! I bet I couldn't do that again if someone paid me to do it." Blake felt pleased.

The captain smiled at Blake's comment then said, "Pull the rope as hard as you can on your end to draw the ship closer to the dock."

Blake gruntingly said, "I'm pulling."

"Careful and steady her."

"We're in now," said Blake. "Drop the anchor and I'll jump out and tie the rest of the ship down."

"Good. Blake. When you're done tying the ropes, see if Mr. DeMarcus is in the coast guard station. I need to ask him about where exactly you need to bury these bones."

"I'm almost done here Dad. But, do I have to go in that ratty place again?"

"Blake, you were there a few weeks ago. You know what it's like, and I'm right here. Nothing is going to happen. I promise."

Blake did not want to disappoint his father. He knew his father was right. He turned and walked slowly toward the coast guard station. He pushed the door open. The sound of the rusty nails echoed in the night. Blake held his stomach tightly. He peered into the dilapidated cabin.

"Mr. DeMarcus, are you in here?" he called out. Blake could see that there was not a soul in sight. He began to tremble remembering the first time he met Mr. DeMarcus. His long-shriveled hands, his long nappy hair, and oh, that fake eye that looked so creepy. The place still reeked of rotting flesh. "Fish I suppose," Blake said in a whisper. He held his breath as-long-as he could. When he couldn't hold it any longer, he ran out the door to meet up with his father. Panting for air, "That coast guard station hasn't gotten any better. It still reeks badly. Dad, I'll help that guy, but he still gives me the creeps. Let's get out of here before he comes back. I don't want to see him," Blake said shaking his head.

Captain deWolfe grabbed Blake by the arm and said, "Blake, hold on. You were fearless for a while. Don't fall back into fear again. Worrying gets you nowhere and paralyzes a person. Don't let it get the best of you."

"Whew." Blake wiped his sweaty forehead with his sleeveless arm, careful not to touch the gash on it. "Can we go now?" Blake questioned.

"Yes!" replied the captain. Blake and his father gathered all the stuff they needed, except the bags of bones. "Those guys are not sleeping at our house. They will stay here tonight until we move them tomorrow," said the captain in disgust. The captain then wrapped his arm around Blake's shoulder, and walked toward their vehicle, silently.

Upon opening the door, Blake felt an excitement come over him that he was leaving this place, at least for tonight. He wanted to sleep in a real bed, and to see his mother whom he missed greatly. They packed up their Hummer. Blake gave a deep yawn, and off they went toward Five Driftwood Lane, to a place called …home. Blake, half awake, entered the huge doorway of the deWolfe mansion unenthusiastically. "We need to make plans where to bury those guys."

The captain looked at Blake and walked toward the library doors. Blake was right behind him. "Careful not to wake your mother," said the captain. He walked over to the fireplace mantel, grabbed his favorite pipe, filled it with cherry tobacco, then struck a match to light it.

Even though Blake wanted to see his mother badly, he said, "I'll stay quiet," while gently closing the huge door behind him.

The library echoed with the jingling of the captain's key chain as he unlocked an oak wood cabinet, the color of honey. Behind the draws were some old maps as well as some newer ones. "They might help Blake in finding a location on where to bury the bones," whispered the captain to himself.

He had hundreds of maps from all over the world. Some were wrapped in special paper to protect them from fraying. He pulled several maps out and placed them onto his desk. "Let's see. Blake, here are some atlases and maps. Look through them. See if you can find where American territory borders on British territory. Like you said earlier, we need to come up with a game plan, only you will have to do the planning.

Remember what DeMarcus said, you will have to be the one all the way. I'm just some muscle in case you need an extra hand. But that's it."

"You're right Dad." Blake picked up a map and examined it. "These maps are very old and look worthless. Do you think they can be of any help, or should I just throw them out?" he said.

"Don't throw anything away. We can't rule them out. Any one of those maps could help us. We simply don't know yet."

The wrinkling of paper echoed in the room. "Dad, would Canada be the closest place that we can go to?" questioned Blake.

"I was hoping you would say that," replied the captain.

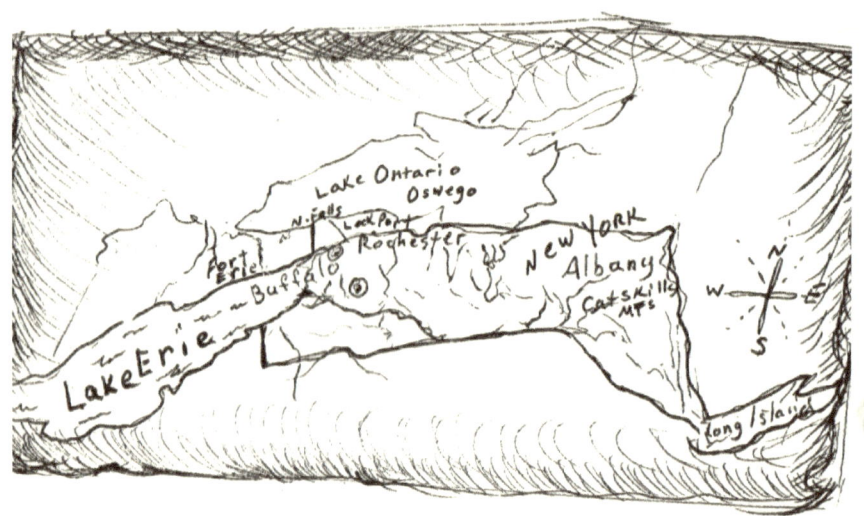

When Blake unraveled the maps, there was another wrapping around them of parchment paper with the date on it. "Hey Dad. Look what I found. Here is a map that is dated in the early 1800s. Canada borders us; North America. It says that Canada was British land at that time. Since the men died during the War of 1812, and Canada was under Britain's rule, then that means we should be able to bury them in Canada, right? And Dad, look. On this map. There's a place called Fort Erie, and it's in Canada. From what I can make out, it looks like it's right across the river from Buffalo, New York.

If that's the case, that means it should be about 600 miles from our house to Buffalo. It should take approximately nine and a half hours to get there."

The captain being impressed by Blake's wisdom, "I knew you would find something in those older maps. That is why I gave them to you. Remember what Mr. DeMarcus said. You must be the mastermind finding them and burying them too. I'm just around for support in any way I can be, including muscle work. Now, take a look to see if your assumptions in location would match a newer map and see if it will have the same route idea you think might take us there."

Time was passing quickly. Blake yawned a healthy one. "Dad, I'm very tired. Can I quit now and turn into my bed? I sure could use the sleep. Besides, in the morning I'll be more up to looking at other maps to pin-point where this fort is."

"I suppose. I'm very tired too. We'll take a cat nap, also check out the road atlas before leaving in the morning."

"Thank heaven." Blake turned and quietly left the library and headed toward his room. The bedroom window was opened. The shear white curtain panels swirled and danced when the wind entered through the screened window. Blake was happy to see his room again. He walked over and sat on the leather chair by the window, overlooking the sea. For once, so relaxed just sitting there, he was just taking in the view and the freshness of the air, not thinking of anything. He did not want to move, for he was physically and mentally exhausted.

Chapter 13: C L O S E D

Blake and the captain rose early the next morning. They skipped breakfast and went directly into the library to find the atlas they needed.

"Is Mom up yet?"

"No. You know your mother. She always thinks ahead. She must've thought we were coming home today. There was a note on her pillow saying she'd gone to Grandma's last night just in case we did come home earlier, which we did.

Blake, disappointed, pouted. "I was hoping to see Mom. I guess a couple of days won't be too long to wait."

After searching one of the maps for a few minutes, Blake cried, "Bingo! Here are some roads that takes you right through Buffalo, New York, across Lake Erie, right into Ontario Canada. Do you think we'll find it in time?" Blake's heart swelled in excitement.

The captain half chuckled at the thought, "We better make it. We came this far, we need to carry the rest of this journey to its completion."

Blake neatly put all the maps back into the honey oak cabinet except the one. He carefully unfolded the huge paper map on the captain's desk. "Okay, let's map out the route, and figure out how long it will really take us to get there." Blake pointed as he mapped out the trip talking it out, "According to the road atlas; we get on the expressway, take the Cross-Island Pkwy, then the Throgs Neck Bridge. We then will have to get on the lower level of the George Washington Bridge to the New Jersey Turnpike, then to the Garden State Parkway. We will have to head toward Scranton, and then exit heading toward Binghamton. After that, we will have to take I-90, to Rt-179 heading toward Blasdell. We've got to get onto Milestrip Rd., and then onto West Lake Shore Rd. Lastly, turn right onto Hover Rd. That will take us all the way to the end of Buffalo, New York. Then we will have to cross over a bridge that goes over Lake Erie into Ontario Canada, in which we will not be so far away from the fort."

"You've done a terrific job, Blake." The captain paused. "You did say we have to cross over a lake, right? Hmm. I do have an inflatable raft in the back of the ship. We'll take it with us upstate in case we need it. With all that we've experienced already, you never know what else can happen. If we get stuck and can't cross the bridge, at least we'll go by raft at that point. But, I hope all goes well. By the way, did you find out approximately how long it will take us to get there?"

"Dad, it sounds like you're waiting for more trouble. Don't scare me." Blake turned to examine the map, "Now, let me see, according to the mile key, it is approximately 600 miles from here like I thought, but not counting crossing the lake and actually locating Fort Erie. That might be another 150 miles. If so, it should take roughly twelve hours by car to get there providing we don't get into a jam."

Captain deWolfe turned to Blake, "I didn't mean to put fear in you; I just want us to be ready for anything." The captain gave a slight pause then continued, "The time is now eight o'clock, and time is precious. We need to gather some necessities to travel north. Go into the shed and get a couple of spades and an extra oar. Take an extra life preserver too. Like I said, you never know—they might come in handy."

Blake left the room, went out the door, and walked down a path using the stepping stones that went through the flower garden over to the wooden shed that resembled a house. Inside he could see that the shovels, rakes, and tools were all hanging in a line like soldiers waiting for a command. The life preservers and oars were in a special box that the captain made to house nautical equipment. On the box was a picture of an anchor and rope that the captain had burnt on with a special tool to make the beautiful markings. Because of the picture, it was easier to find and to know what was in it. Blake picked out items quickly and dropped them beside the Hummer that was waiting on the blue-stoned lined driveway. He reentered the house, "Okay Dad, we're ready. Let's go now before the traffic gets heavy." Blake seemed to have more years on him because of the things he knew, and experienced, then just being twelve years old. The captain and Blake locked up the house and headed toward the driveway. They threw everything into the vehicle, and off they went to where the Guerriere was docked.

They drove up a long dirt path that was outlined with tall trees, some not so nice, to reach the parking lot where the docks were. Both opened their doors of the vehicle at the same time, then Blake went over to the back of it to open the hatchback ready to place more necessities from the Guerriere itself.

Blake and his father walked over to the ship. Hanging over the side of the ship was a ladder. Blake took hold of it. Holding on tightly, he climbed the loose rope ladder onto the ship's deck. He searched for the inflatable raft, oars, and life preservers. He found them in a wooden box with the same markings just like the one the captain made at home. Blake dragged what he needed to the side of the ship, and threw the raft overboard first, then the other things on top, being careful not to break anything. He then searched for the burlap bags that held the skeletons. He carried them from the hold of the ship, that was below the deck, and to the side of the vessel. Blake grabbed one of the bone rattling bags and hurled it toward the captain. "Catch, Dad!" Then the other twelve followed. "This is the quickest way to take everything we needed off this ship," said Blake. When he was done, he climbed down the rungs of the ladder. He headed toward Captain deWolfe where he was placing the last bag with the others beside the vehicle. Looking around, they swiftly laid the bags in the back of the Hummer, hoping that no one had seen them.

Blake said, "Dad, I'm so nerved up."

"Try not to think about it. Hurry. Get in the truck."

"What if someone saw us? What if they call the cops? Do you think we'll be arrested?"

"Blake, no one knows what's in those bags other than you and I."

"Yeah, but maybe we look suspicious to people."

The captain grinned. "Blake. There weren't many people by their boats this morning. Relax. No one saw us."

Blake bit his bottom lip. "I hope you're right Dad."

The Hummer pulled away down the dirt road, and just at that moment Blake's eyes bulged at a park policeman that passed them by on his way to the harbor. Blake went into a frenzy at the sight of the oncoming car. Blake jerking his arms around, "I knew it! They're coming to get us! Dad we're gonna get arrested! I just knew it!"

Captain deWolfe lurched his arm toward his son, "Blake, take it easy. Your making yourself sick. We haven't done anything wrong. Besides, that's park police, not county police. The park police keep an eye on the docks. He is patrolling the area, that's all."

Blake wiped his furrowed brow. "Whew. I feel stupid now. I guess I let my imagination get the best of me, didn't I?"

"I would say so. But don't say you're stupid. I would be nervous too, only I know the job of the park police. I'm always around them.' The captain threw the newspaper at Blake. "Here. Now, recline your seat and read a bit, or rest while I drive. We have a long way to go."

"I'm calm now, Dad. Honest. I don't need to rest, but I'll read instead."

The captain gazed at his gas gauge. "Before we go onto the expressway, I need to gas up." He pulled into the gas station, pulled out his gas credit card from his wallet, and gave it to Blake then said, "Here's my card. Tell the man you want a fill up."

Blake's eyes widened and replied, "As long as there are no policemen around."

The captain laughed out loud. "Blake, we'll be all right. I promise you that." Somehow Blake knew it would be okay when the captain would say. "I promise."

After Blake gassed up, they headed west, traveling for hours. Traffic on the expressway, turnpikes and thruways were heavy. "There is no way we are making it in twelve hours," said Blake impatiently. "It took so long just to get out of New York City."

"Keep your fingers crossed that we are able to bury these skeletons before the time DeMarcus gave us expires. We have twenty-eight hours left," said the captain. At the mention of DeMarcus, Blake cringed.

Time passed, and night had fallen. Blake and his father were exhausted from traveling, and not having enough sleep the night before.

Traveling on I-90, Captain deWolfe blinked hard behind the wheel. "Blake, I have to pull over. I can't see where I'm going anymore. I need to rest my eyes."

"Sure Dad. I guess we still have some time after all. Once we got out of the city, unexpectedly the traffic got much less. To tell you the truth, I wouldn't mind closing my eyes too," Blake said with a yawn.

That night the air was warm, and the moon shone bright. The captain found a safe spot to pull over on the side of the road. "We'll rest here for a while." The captain opened the windows halfway to let the moving night air rush in. They both reclined their seats, and immediately both dozed off to dream land.

Still in the truck, at dawn, Blake's sleep was disrupted by loud sounds of huge flapping wings, and heavy gusts of wind. He thought he was dreaming when he heard his name being called once again. All too real to Blake, his eyes opened wide, his heart pounded in his chest. He sat up and whispered, "No-no. You can't do this," he replied to what he thought he heard. *I couldn't have really heard those voices*, he tried reasoning to himself. *I didn't hear them for a long time, and I couldn't have heard them now. No. I must still be asleep.*

"*B-L-A-K-E, B-L-A-K-E, you must set us free, B-L-A-K-E.*" The voices twirled in the wind and gave a frightening echo in Blake's ears.

Blake held his head. He shouted at the lurking voices. "I did set you free! I set you free when I risked my own life and my father's life to find you in the bottom of that Ghost Ship! Leave me alone. Stop bothering me!"

The captain jumped out of his sleep. "Blake, who are you fighting with?"

"The voices, Dad. They started all over again. I can't believe those spirits are bothering me again. Can we just leave those sacks out here in the woods? I don't want to drive with them in the truck." Blake trembled as he spoke.

"No. We can't do that. Blake, it's going to be okay.' The captain patted Blake's head, then straightened himself up. He searched his pocket for the important element to get them out of there. Pulling them out of his pant pocket, he found the one he needed and put the key in the ignition and drove off. "Blake, are you sure you've heard the voices?'

"Dad, I'm as sure of it as I see and hear you now,' he said in despair.

"How much time do we have?'

"We have until six thirty tonight. Do you think we'll make it or will we be hindered by some craziness?'

"We should, providing that we fight through whatever comes against us quickly."

"B-L-A-K-E, B-L-A-K-E, B-L-A-K-E,' continued the screeching voices. Breathing heavily, Blake covered his ears with both fists, and between his teeth he pleaded, "Dad, please make them stop!'

The captain glanced at his son. "Blake. Listen to me. I think once they are buried, you won't hear them again.'

"They hurt my ears. Please make them stop," he continued.

"Just hang in there. I'll try to get there as fast as I can.'

Driving a few hours up through Buffalo, they found at the base of the bridge orange flashing lights, and a long wooden barrier in the middle of the road. On it was a sign that spelled **C-L-O-S-E-D** in bold, black lettering. Blake's heart shattered like glass being struck with a hammer. "Should we try to go around another way?'

"No. That would take too long. Thank goodness we brought the raft. I'll find the shore and park the Hummer. We'll have to launch out and chance going across."

"*B-L-A-K-E, now. Quickly B-L-A-K-E*," said the terrifying voices again. Blake feeling troubled, jumped up and down throwing his arms in every direction. "All right! I'm on my way, you stupid hideous voices! Can't you see we're almost there?" The veins popped out of his neck as he shouted.

The captain spoke calmly in trying to put his son at ease, "No, Blake. They can't see. They are dead, but restless because they aren't buried yet and that is what they are communicating to you. They need their final resting place."

Blake turned his head and spotted the lake they had to cross. He pointed impatiently toward it. "Dad, hurry and park the truck over there in the clearance at the edge of the lake. I'll get out, grab the raft and inflate it not to waste time."

"*B-L-A-K-E, B-L-A-K-E, B-L-A-K-E!*" The pitch was so sharp; it pierced Blake's ears. He held his hands tightly to his ears, wanting to cry.

"Dad, my ear is bleeding!"

The captain pulled out a tissue from the box on the dashboard and handed it to Blake. "Here. Put this over your ear for now. We need to move fast, real fast, and don't lose heart. We're almost at the end of this diabolical thing that gripped you for weeks."

The captain slammed on his brakes in the middle of a section of tall grass and reeds but cleared enough to park. They both jumped out. Still in pain, Blake immediately got the rubber raft out, pulled the pin and instantly it inflated. Meanwhile, the captain got the oars, the spades and the dead men's bones out of the vehicle.

Blake dragged the raft into the water. The captain swiftly flung the oars and the bags into it, then Blake jumped in holding onto the spades balancing himself and being careful not to tear the rubber raft. He wedged the bags under his seat, and then wedged the spades between the burlap bags, cautiously. The captain gave the raft a healthy push then jumped in too. Captain deWolfe began to row what looked like the never-ending lake.

"*B-L-A-K-E, B-L-A-K-E, H-U-R-R-Y B-L-A-K-E!*"

"I can't take those voices anymore!" Blake's eyes gushed out hot tears that ran down his face. He put his hands over his eyes and sobbed. "Dad, I can't take it anymore," he said in a slur, while his shoulders jerked up and down. He felt he was going insane.

The captain rowed frantically, "You can do it son, hang in there. You're almost done with this horror forever."

Halfway across the lake, a raging storm came, creating white squalls on the water. "Hold on! I've never seen this before. I didn't know white squalls were possible on a lake." The rubber raft flew up into the air, and crashed back down, almost capsizing it. "We've lost an oar!" shouted the captain. "Can you see the bags, Blake?"

"Yeah. They're still wedged under the seat." Blake looked around for the life preservers. His eyes widened in horror. More fear gripped his heart. "Dad! We were in such a hurry that we forgot to bring the preservers! Now what?"

"This is where you put to action what you've learned in Sunday school. Depend on the Man up above to bring us out of this mess. He's been with us from the start; He'll see us through to the very end."

"*B-L-A-K-E, S-A-V-E US.*"

"I'm trying to save myself. Don't you understand? You're dead! I'm still alive!"

"We're almost there. Hang in there Blake and hold on. Here comes another big wave." The raft rose up and fell. One of the bags escaped from under the seat, and the two spades. All three went flying into the air, then splash, right into the water.

"Noooo! Nooo!" cried Blake. Without giving it much thought, he dove in after the sack, not caring about losing the spades at all.

"Blake! What are you doing?" The captain quickly stuck out one of the oars, "Here, grab the oar!"

Blake did not listen. "I have to find the bag!" He dove deep into the water. He fought with heavy seaweed, pushing them out of his way. He reached for the sack as it sunk quickly but lost it.

Captain deWolfe jumped to his feet on the raft shouting out for Blake, "Come back! As Captain of this vessel, I command you to come back!" Blake kicked his feet and arms in every direction to steady his swimming action. After a while, a stream of bubbles escaped from his nose. I'm losing my breath, he thought, And where is that sack? I've got to find it. I won't return until I do! He swam the opposite way and right behind him was the sack sinking faster and faster. He went after it, squinting not to get seaweed into his eyes.

"Blake!" the captain continued to shout over the rough water.

After a couple of long minutes, Blake's hand popped up from the tormented water, holding the sack, then his head came up right after shaking his drenched hair from his eyes. "Dad!! Throw me the oar!" he shouted desperately, gasping for air.

The captain jumped quickly to reach for the oar and threw it overboard toward Blake, catching him right on the head. "Hold on 'til I get there." With the other oar, the captain anxiously made his way toward Blake. "Here, grab hold of my arm. I'm going to pull you in."

Blake, in pain and still holding onto the burlap bag, said to his father, "I couldn't let that bag go down. I've made it this far. I'm going to finish what I came out to do."

They gained more courage from each other as they rode out the sudden storm, and by a miracle, made it to the other side. What will await them on the Canadian side the rest of the way is for now an unknown journey to them.

Chapter 14: Grave Yard and Bon-Voyage

Blake and the captain had reached the border of Canada. They carried the burlap sacks off the raft and hid the plastic vessel in a patch of reed and tall grass. The captain suggested placing one bag inside the other, so he could hike with them better. They walked along the shore, heading east for two miles. There, by the water's edge was a stone coast guard station painted brilliant white. It looked warm, cozy and inviting. It was charming, not like the one the Guerriere was docked at.

Captain deWolfe slowed down his pace and pointed straight ahead. "Hay. Look. Signs of life. Let's stop there to see if anyone can tell us where Fort Erie is located." They walked around the station made of stone and luckily, they found a man who looked like a cabdriver. "I hope he doesn't ask too many questions when I talk to him," mumbled the captain toward Blake. "Uh, excuse me. Can you tell me where Fort Erie is? And, can you direct me to one who might drive a cab?" the captain asked a man who was sitting at a table drinking coffee and finishing a pastry.

"I'm a cabbie," said the man wrinkling his forehead with a slight accent, while examining the captain up and down. He took the last sip of his coffee then spoke, "Fourt Yerie You say? Dhat's a chost town now. No-one goes to Fourt Yerie. Dhat place has not been used in years, Sir."

"Can you take us there?" the captain asked.

The cabdriver took off his black leather cap, scratched his bald head, and turned back to the captain. "You know, people say dhat place is haunted."

"But can you take us there?" the captain persisted.

"I suppose.' The cabbie put money on the table and went outside. Blake and his father followed him. "What you've got dhere?" asked the driver pointing to the sacks.

"Oh, our personal things, that's all," replied the captain, looking at Blake hoping he doesn't say anything. Blake began to have the worried look. The captain added, "Blake, we're going to take this cab to Fort Erie. Hop in."

Before Blake took one step the driver said, "Wait a minute." Blake froze and stared at his father. The driver got out of the cab and walked toward Blake. Blake feeling nervous, reached for his stomach. The driver went over to the back of the cab and opened the trunk. "Here, put your stuff in here," demanded the cab driver. "Dhere will be more ruum for you."

Blake gave a sigh of relief and placed the burlap sacks quickly and carefully into the trunk. He chose to sit in the back seat, away from the stranger. He opened the door and jumped right in before his father could suggest him sitting up front. Entering the cab, the driver asked, "You travel much?"

"Yes, we do," the captain replied.

The driver turned the ignition on, then put the cab into gear, and drove off toward Fort Erie. "Wat brings you here?" asked the driver.

"Oh, a little sight-seeing. My son and I are into history, so we've decided to visit some old places—you know—just for the heck of it."

While in the cab, Blake heard the voices again, and again, and again. "*B-L-A-K-E SAVE US!*" They continued with a screeching, ear-piercing cry for help.

Blake did not dare say a word. His heart beat fast like a music timer ticking away. He could hear from the back seat the rattling of the bones that were in the trunk as they drove through the unsettled pavement. Blake began to wonder if the stranger could hear it too. He glared out the window, biting his lip, hoping that would get his mind off his hurting ear, and the voices that kept tormenting him. Suddenly, his eyes filled with tears. Blake thought, I couldn't give away our secret. I can't, and I won't. He closed his eyes tightly, while his head bounced on the cab's window. He wiped the warm wet stream from his cheeks. When he opened his eyes, he saw an abandoned place at the end of a dirt road with a sign that read, "Fort Erie" in faded lettering swinging on a nail.

"Here we are," said the cabdriver. He drove through the broken, rusted, black iron gates with gargoyle heads on top of two poles that added to its already creepiness.

"Thank goodness we're here," was all Blake said.

The man stopped the vehicle and shifted it into park. "Dhat will be fifteen Canadian dollars," he said with his arm extended, and his palm facing the sky.

The captain reached into his damp wallet, "I only have American money. Here is thirty dollars. Keep the change."

"Dhanks a lot Sir!" he said staring at the money. The square-jawed man tipped his hat and ran to the back of the cab to open the trunk with a great big smile.

Blake immediately followed the cab driver to fetch the sacks from the place where they were lying, while Captain deWolfe kept the stranger busy by talking. The bags rattled as Blake pulled them out to lay them on the ground. Thank goodness the cab driver did not pay any mind to what Blake was doing.

After the stranger left, Blake and the captain picked up the burlap bags and walked toward the back of an abandoned log cabin.

Blake was astonished when he spotted a huge burial ground in the back of the building. He read some of the tombstones. Some were army soldiers, and others were sailors who had died in war throughout the centuries. The graveyard wasn't all that manicured, but not terribly overgrown with foliage and weeds either. It looked like a grave keeper came around every now and then to keep it from overgrowing immensely.

"Dad. This is unbelievable." Blake was thrilled there was a graveyard in sight. "We need to find a spot to bury these sacks," he said looking for a perfect spot. "I can't believe we lost all our spades in the water during that crazy storm. We'll have to look around until we find something to dig with," as he was talking his eyes searched the ground hoping to find something—anything at all.

While pointing, the captain spoke, "Look around in the grass. Look over there by the log cabin too. You might get lucky."

Blake searched the east end of the grounds for a few minutes, while Captain deWolfe searched the west. "Did you find anything yet, Dad?"

"No. Not yet."

"I'm going by the cabin now." As Blake got near the cabin, he tripped over a stick and fell on his hands, "Ouch!" he blurted out looking at one hand with a small, deep gash.

"Are you all right, Blake?"

"Yeah! I just tripped over something in the grass, that's all." Blake got up and traced the grassy stick with his fingers, hoping to find a pointed edge. "It's a shovel!" shouted Blake in good spirits.

The captain feeling joyful also at the find, laughed a hardy laugh forgetting for a moment the anguish they were about to witness. "Great, bring it here and I'll start digging. Maybe you can trip over another one," said the captain playfully.

Blake couldn't find anything funny in his father's comment. He shoved the foliage out of his way and examined the ground once again. After a few minutes, he found a broken shovel in the front of the deserted log cabin, under some shrubs. "Dad, I found one. It's broken, but it still would work." "Good. Come help me dig."

Blake remembered what DeMarcus had said about the thirteen dead men's bones. "Uh, Dad, remember what Mr. DeMarcus said—I had to bury them?"

The captain looked up at Blake. "I can help you dig. It's muscle work. I know you will have to handle each bag, putting them in the hole, then the soil on top of them. Technically, you would be burying them," said the captain hoping he was right. It was worth a chance so that he could bury each one before the allotted time was up. "So, let's get to digging." The moment of being a bit tenderhearted ended abruptly.

The captain and Blake dug what it seemed to be hours at high speed. Their muscles burned and ached from the strain. Hole, after hole, after hole was dug up. After digging the tenth hole the captain asked, "What time is it?"

"Wow. It's six o'clock. We still have three more holes to dig. Do you think we can make it? I'm exhausted already," replied Blake.

"I know we don't have much left in us, but it'll have to be enough. Only time will tell if we can pull it off." The captain began to doubt himself but didn't give Blake a glimpse of it.

Blake's hands were blistered from digging, and his face and arms were red from the sun, but he did not stop. He understood that the only way to break the chains of mental torment was to bury the bones of the thirteen men. His muscles throbbed even more than before from being over worked. His clothes were drenched with sweat. After the last hole was dug, one burlap sack after another, all in a row, were set in place. Blake used his hands as a shovel and swept the dirt over each one. He didn't care if the dirt stung and filled the gash he had or his opened, blistered wounds. Anything was better than the mental anguish he was going through. It was now one minute to half past six when the last sack was finally buried. They both were muddied from head to toe.

Breathing heavily, the captain wiped his brow with his soiled hands. "I can't believe it. We made it," said the captain practically in tears.

"That was a close one," Blake spoke with a slur. "But we did do it. I hope it is over for good now," Blake continued, breathless. He turned to his father, "Dad, I think they stopped. I don't hear them anymore. And my ear, it doesn't hurt as much."

Feeling exhausted and lifeless, Blake and his father slumped over the top of the last victim's grave. "Thank God it's over," Blake said barely getting the words out of his mouth; on his way crashing into a deep sleep, and so did the captain. They stayed there all night.

Blake awoke at five-thirty the next morning, disoriented. He shook his head and thought he'd been having another nightmare. Every muscle ached. He struggled to reach over to the captain. He shook his head and said, "Wake up. We've got to get out of here before someone finds us out."

Wiping the sleep from their eyes, the two hopped to their feet when a sudden shifting of the ground was felt, then a terrible rumble. Both fell to the ground. "What is happening! An earthquake?" Blake cried out. Then to their frightful surprise, they both witnessed all the graves that Blake covered with soil, had the nameplates that Blake had found on board The Ghost Ship and put them in each man's burlap bag. "How did the nameplates get out of the ground?" Blake questioned, but truly didn't want an answer. "Let's get the heck out of here! I'm done. Soo-done!"

Without thinking twice, they hurried back to the direction they came from. No calling for a cab this time. They didn't want anyone seeing them the way they looked and having to explain anything. Thirsty and hungry, they walked for many miles to where their raft was. They sat for several minutes not saying a word. Then Blake went over to the patch of high swamp grass and pulled out the raft and the two oars and dragged them to the water. He jumped in the raft first, and the captain gave it a good push, and hopped in after. Blake finally broke silence, "I'm glad before we left home that you told me to bring an extra oar, because we ended up losing one." The captain gave a half smile.

Even though their bodies were in pain, Blake and the captain took turns rowing across what seemed to be, the endless lake. The lake itself was calm, and smooth as glass. That day, it was easy sailing across the water. When they reached the other side, there was the magnificent Hummer, just as they left it waiting for them to enter it. It was a fine sight for very sore eyes. Blake deflated the raft, opened the trunk and struggled to throw it in, followed by the two oars. Blake and his father entered the truck, and off they went. The drive took them into the night. It seemed it took longer to get back to Greenville Seaport where the Guerriere was docked than the trip had been from Greenville Seaport to Canada.

As they pulled up, the headlights of the Hummer shone toward Mr. DeMarcus. They saw him dressed in a dusty wool high collar, navy blue coat with tails holding a lantern, and saw a dull shine of its *entire* collection of gold buttons in place. His tan breeches were filthy and torn. He wore faded black leather boots up to his knees. The captain quickly put his truck in park, then rushed out to intercept the man, but it was too late. He was already going on board the Guerriere, the ship that Captain deWolfe bought from him just a few weeks ago.

Blake checked his pocket one more time for the gold button that looked like the ones on DeMarcus' coat, but it was gone. It was one minute to midnight. "Bon Voyage!" shouted Mr. DeMarcus, waving his bony hand. "And thank ye for freedom!"

Blake couldn't believe his eyes. The ship pulled away from the dock in full sail. After one minute of sailing, the Guerriere seemed to turn old. The new canvas sails that Captain deWolfe had mounted on the masts grew old and tattered. The great ship disappeared into a thick, fogbound night with Mr. DeMarcus on it.

Blake and the captain looked at each other, too stunned to say a word, too tired to do anything. The captain slid to the ground and sat still with his mouth open for several minutes. "Blake," he said, "I think I finally saw what you've been talking about all this time."

"Yes, Dad. You did."

"The ship I bought a few weeks ago was never to be mine in the first place. It truly was a ghost ship; only I couldn't recognize it. Because of your courage, all this was designed for you to find and bury those skele-

tons, so they could finally find rest. After two-hundred years, they are at peace now."

Neither of them said a word for the next few minutes, then Blake broke the silence, "Come on Dad. I think it's time to go home." Blake took his father by the arm, helped him off the ground, walked him toward the Hummer, and helped him in. Blake put himself in the Hummer too. It took half-an-hour before the captain could move to put the vehicle into gear.

The next evening, at home, Blake was still tired from all he's gone through. He went down to the seashore below his house. Feeling sleepy, he sat on the sand, against a boulder. Beginning to doze off he heard, "*Blake. Blake,*" in the wind. He felt spiking pain go through his chest and felt faint. He held his breath and opened his eyes slowly. He could feel his blood run cold in the warm night.

He looked over his shoulder and saw a shadow in the distance. Blake gave a sigh of relief, realizing it was his mom. Thank God. "Coming!" he shouted. Blake got to his feet, put on his water shoes, and ran up the sixty-six splintering wooden steps, past the towering blue spruce toward home, to sleep in his own bed. And what a great night of sleep it was.

Agnes Rodriguez Contes was born in 1957 in Brooklyn and raised on Long Island, New York. It was hard growing up in the 60s being Hispanic, until she met Jesus for her own. He gave her the strength to face and overcome the challenges of life. Today, she and her husband Johnny have three married children and four grandchildren. She is involved with home schooling her grandchildren and has a degree in English, from SUNY Empire State College. She  has studied with The Institute of Children Literature in Connecticut.

This book came to be during a family camping trip. One day at the beach, half the sea had an eerie mist, and half the sea was sunny. The Misty side had a barge far off--the Ghost Ship--and the rest is history. The purpose of this Historical Fiction is to spark a love of reading with adventure for the reluctant reader. The non-stop action draws the reader in and does not let go. There are historical facts in the beginning and a bibliography at the end to spark one's own research.

Sources for Ghost Warship of 1812

Selected Naval Documents USS CONSTITUTION. "Engagement with HMS Guerriere,1812." Department of the Navy-Naval Historical Center. 805 Kidder Breese SE--Washington Navy Yard Washington DC 20374-5060. 16 March, 2002. http://www.history.navy.mil/docs/war1812/const5.htm

Barnes, James. Naval Actions of the War of 1812. New York: Harper and Brothers Publishers, 1896.

Berton, Pierre. The Invasion of Canada 1812-1813. Canada: A Penguin Book, 1988.

Bosco, Peter. The War of 1812. Brookfield Connecticut: The Millbrook Press, 1991.

Carter, Alden. The War of 1812. USA: F.B., 1993.

Druett, Joan. Hen Frigates Wives of Merchant Captains Under Sail. Rockefeller Center, 1230 Ave. pf the Americas, New York, NY 10020: Simon and Schuster, 1998.

Greenblatt, Miriam. America at War: The War of 1812. 460 Park Ave. South, New York, NY 10016: Facts on File, 1994.

Horsman, Reginald. The War of 1812. USA: A Borzoi Books, Published by Alfred. A Knopf. Inc., 1969.

Mahon, John. The War of 1812. Gainesville: University of Florida Press, 1972.

Roosevelt, Theodore. The Naval War of 1812. 27 and 29 West 23rd Street, New York: G.P. Putnam's Sons, third edition, 1883.

Student Atlas of the World. Editorial Office at 77 Central Street, Boston, Massachusetts 02109, Published in the US: Charles E. Tuttle Company Inc., 1993.

www.ingramcontent.com/pod-product-compliance
Lightning Source LLC
Chambersburg PA
CBHW030531080526
44586CB00011B/392